The Bible On Miracles

The Bible

on

Miracles

by A. De GROOT, S.V.D.

Translated by JOS. A. ROESSEN, S.C.J.

ST. NORBERT ABBEY PRESS
De Pere, Wisconsin
U. S. A.
1966

Biblical quotations are from the Revised Standard Version of the Bible, copyrighted 1946 and 1952 by the Division of Christian Education, National Council of Churches, and used by permission.

Nihil obstat:

Samuel D. Jadin, O. Praem.
Censor deputatus

Imprimatur: 163486

†Stanislaus V. Bona, D.D.
Bishop of Green Bay
April 13, 1966

Originally published as
De Bijbel over het Wonder
Roermond and Maaseik, J. J. Romen & Zonen, 1961

Library of Congress catalogue card number: 66 - 22818

Printed in the United States of America
ST. NORBERT ABBEY PRESS
De Pere, Wisconsin

CONTENTS

We constantly use the word "miracle" and we use it with careless ease. The whole world speaks, for example, of the German **Wirtschaftswunder:** how the West German Republic, after World War II, was able, in record time, to reach a status of affluence and to make a substantial contribution to the political, economic and cultural reconstruction of Europe, thus playing a significant role on the international stage. We daily witness the "miracles" of technology and are surprised that human endeavor achieves things which a short time ago seemed impossible. If suddenly and contrary to all expectation we are saved from a very difficult situation, we call it a miracle or if we see the fulfillment of a wish we ourselves were unable to accomplish and which now, as a gratuitous gift, is placed in our lap. Finally, we regard a work of art which has reached perfection and manifests the genius of its maker as a miracle.

Such usage of the word — we feel this instinctively — is rather casual; we are uneasy when faced with a real miracle because — and we are indeed conscious of this — a miracle has something to do with God. He is, in one way or another, part of the definition. As long as he is not involved, one cannot speak of a real miracle. Because the miracle that points to God points also to our own hearts, one who sees a work of God simultaneously becomes to some extent more conscious of himself. Is it not possible that this is precisely where we must seek the reason why man is so opposed to miracles? Is it not because he prefers to be left out, to be left in peace? In stark contrast to this one finds a weak reluctance for contact with the mysterious or the miraculous, for attention given to a miracle-doctor or charlatan, for searching into the occult, for the desire to associate with mysterious powers. Outside the Church we notice this in the pretensions of astrology, fortune-telling and spiritualism; these are forms of superstition which, as a pseudo-religion, supply a need. Within the Church are many who look for apparitions, prophecies and apocalyptic sensations; we find devotees and fanatics who court messages from heaven and display an unhealthy anxiety to discover a new message destined for our time.

For these reasons it is well to question the meaning of miracle. It is important to do this from Holy Scripture itself. We look in vain for a scientific definition of miracle in the Bible; on the other hand we do feel its meaning, and this is precisely why we tend to avoid conversation about miracles or even are tempted to try to reason them out of existence scientifically; we do feel the religious reality they represent, and the divine appeal which stems from them.

The Bible is not concerned with the question what a miracle is from the point of view of natural science or philosophy. It does not try to place it within the ambit of the natural order. It presents only what God means it to be in relation to man. Here the real essence of the miracle is to be sought. To pursue this, as presented in the Bible, is the purpose of this exposition.

MIRACLES AND THE HISTORY
OF SALVATION IN THE
OLD TESTAMENT

1. A widespread but incomplete view of miracles

Anyone who has studied Biblical History with visual aids will certainly remember that the Old Testament is a book with many wonderful stories and that God is active in it as One not to be mocked. The ten plagues of Egypt were not so strange, except for the death of the firstborn; it was apparent that the Egyptian magicians were able to bring about quite formidable results too. The Passage through the Red Sea and the destruction of Pharaoh's army were very impressive, but our expositor found a solution in the turning tide, so familiar to us on the North Sea shore, which bares the beach and covers it again. Most intriguing was the story of Elias on Mount Carmel in his battle against the idolatrous priests and the presumption, it seems to us, with which he called for a miracle; the idea frightens us. What a catastrophe it would have been if he had lost. Luckily for him and for us, he won.

When reading again, years later, it became appar-

ent that the story teller, in trying to be convincing,
had outdone even the pictures. Is it surprising then
that one asks if the narrator of the Bible might not
have added to the story here and there? This brought
about a critical inclination to reduce everything to
the minutest detail of historical event. This was
done to show that here was a well-adjusted thinking
human being; it was done especially so that one
would not lose faith in the Bible.

In the meantime there was a development of the
insight that to reduce everything to the minutest
detail of historical event was to start at the wrong
end. This was not just because one missed the
point completely, but because it is more important
to start with the faith of the prophet and the people;
they interpreted these physical occurrences in a
special historical context. But before we finish we
should add a little about the sincere passion for
historical truth which motivates us when we read the
Bible. It is clear that a certain reality must be the
basis for a description of the miraculous. This we
do not doubt; the faith of the prophet and the
people is founded on it. We are inquisitive and we
ask: Exactly what happened? The Bible leaves us
at a loss. Why? Because we look upon the miracle
in a different way, demanding something from it
and wanting to prove something which is obvious
in the Bible.

How do **we** look upon miracles?[1] A miracle is
related to the unusual. But this unusual is such that
it means a transgression of the "natural" possibilities

present. The miracle then becomes a fact, an occurrence which cannot be explained from given natural
conditions at that certain moment; it consequently
points to a cause which must be outside and above
these conditions. But even then this is not enough.
The "outside" and "above" must be realized in a
radical sense: a cause which is transcendent outside
and above everything that is of this world. This
cause must, demonstrably, be God, and can be only
God. The concept "nature" acts as criterion for
judgment and determination of a miracle. This concept, with which we are familiar through philosophy
and natural science, has had an immense influence on
the present-day notion of God, especially for many
Christians. By "nature" we mean the total visible
reality around us, which constitutes in itself a closed
and rounded totality which moves through its own
vitality and conforms to its own laws and norms.
Whatever does not result from this is therefore called
"outside" or "supernatural." This statement does
not deny, as is obvious to a Christian, that God has
a hand in the minutest events in nature. But this does
not exclude that the laws of natural phenomena
discovered through science, and the still-growing
knowledge of the causes which determine the natural
process, might make man suppose that everything
follows its course in such way that no God is needed
in the process. This has tempted many to place
God outside the event and to see him only as having
created the world — as having started the machine
which now runs itself. Still more fatal is the conclusion that the world is so governed and enclosed by

its laws that no single outside causality can determine
the process of nature. A breakthrough of the divine
into the world appertains therefore to the realm of
impossibilities. Thus comes denial first of the fact
and then of the possibility of God's activities within
the world. Miracles are disqualified as contrary to
nature by reason of the unalterable and unbreakable
"laws of nature" which one observes. This raises
many objections from Catholic quarters. The miracle
(wonder) does not abrogate the laws of nature and
does not destroy the order of the world. The existence of the world — the world in which a multitude
of vital processes are at work — is a continuous
"becoming" in the hand of God. Its existence is a
lasting reality and thus, in the manner of its existence,
it is a becoming-created. God remains ever faithful
to his own creation; so, in a miracle, he lets created
causes cooperate **with** the miracle, through communication of powers that act within the sphere
of nature. It is apparent in many miracles that they
bring the laws of nature to light in an entirely new
way. Thus miraculous cures do not, as a rule,
transgress the possibilities of a natural cure; they
advance and force the process in a way that pre-
sumes for the powers present a higher capacity than
would normally be expected. Thus the miracle shows
itself integrated into a higher totality of activities.
But one may not assume that it is merely added to
existing creation from the outside. It is a realization
of in-the-world-present potentialities according to
its own laws but in such a way that the combination
arising would be impossible through its own forces

at that particular moment. Although the miracle is an exception to what is expected, it is also true in regard to its recognition, that God rules the world according to laws proper to it. The miracle as God's initiative, in its execution, conforms minutely to the world's order without contradicting it.

The unexpectedness of the miracle, its shock effect on routine observation, can lead more easily than the normal course of things to the question: Is there possibly a meaning behind this extraordinary happening? Catholic theology has asked this question for centuries. Answers have been varied. The last two centuries have been so preoccupied with an apologetic defense against the allegations of natural philosophy and sciences that the problem — how and if the miracle can prove divine revelation — has filled the entire field of polemics concerning miracles. Compelled by necessity, theologians made demands on miracles which could apply as necessary conditions to prove that God, and only he, could have had a hand in these extraordinary events. Quite firmly, they demanded that the miracle should surpass every natural explanation; in addition, they claimed that it could never be explained naturally. They smuggled conditions into the definition which they decidedly asserted belong to the essence of miracles. This conviction was so obvious that they never asked if these conditions were possibly related only to the evidential impact assigned to the miracle, rather than to the miracle itself.

It is not our task to analyze this further. Our only

purpose in mentioning this is to indicate a generally
accepted theory which has strongly influenced the
reading of the Bible. From this point of view the
miracles mentioned in the Bible were tested exclusively on the basis of their apologetic usefulness;
they were evaluated from this point of view. Consequently, there has been a continuing attempt to
acquire apologetic certainty about all aspects of the
occurrences. Certainty as to whether or not an event
could still be called a miracle depended on this;
because this certainty was more often than not
problematical, the number of miracles was reduced
and the miraculous whittled down to left-over and
accepted facts. Such a theory is foreign to the
writers of the Bible.

2. The Biblical viewpoint of miracles

Anyone who tries to find the Biblical concept of
miracles from a lexicon or concordance and how
this can comprehensibly be put into words, will be
disappointed. Quest for miracles and their meaning
seems to be a difficult task. The usage of the word
makes this immediately clear. In all the miracle
narratives in Scripture, the word that would coincide
with our word "wonder" or "miracle," is seldom used
in the original text. In all these cases very different
terms are used. There are less nuances in our translations than in the Biblical original — perhaps even
still less in more modern translations. Word statistics
and derivations are not much help. If we want to
know what underlies Scripture's inclusion of miraculous events, we must look for other realities

which form or directly determine their background.

a. Miracles and physical order

Let us limit ourselves first to the relationship between miracles and the physical order. Does the Bible have the same concept we do? No; the concept "nature," as shown above, is unknown in Scripture; consequently "transgression of natural limits," as we understand it is also unknown. The Bible never presents a miracle-nature relation; it presents the miracle-God relation. The miracle is, in the Bible, an experience of God's activity in events.[2]

According to the Scriptural viewpoint, everything that exists is invariably God's work: the starry sky and the earth, the sea and the continents, the flora and fauna and man (Gen. 1). The world owes its existence to God; it depends on him for its continued being and all that is performed in it. The sacred writer makes God rest from his work at the end of his creation (Gen. 2:2), not to suggest that from now on he would not move a finger for his creation, but to urge upon man the commandment to rest in his work cycle and to adore God. Jesus' word in John 5:17: "My Father is working still" underlines what is experienced in all of Scripture. In the Biblical sense, God is the living, actively working, omnipotent, self-revealing God. His power is the source of all vitality on earth. Everything that happens here leads back to God as to origin and source. Thus he is, above all, the direct-acting force in all physical and biological phenomena we observe. "He sends forth his commands to the earth; his word runs swiftly. He gives snow like wool, he scatters hoar-frost like ashes. He casts forth his ice like morsels; who can stand before his cold? He sends forth his word and melts them; he makes his wind blow and the waters flow" (Ps. 147:15-18).

It is he who sends rain and holds it back (Amos 4:7-8), who makes the harvest prosper or not (Hosea 2:9). He holds life and death in his hand (Ps. 22:10; 90:3; 104:29; Job 10:8) and effects the fruitfulness of offspring (Gen. 21:1-2; 29:31; 49:25; 1 Sam. 1). In short, all that occurs does so through him, obeying his commanding word. This word is not limited, it is omnipotent. Nothing is too difficult for Yahweh (Gen. 18:14), no work is too great (Jer. 32:17).

The regularity with which natural phenomena follow each other and recur is not ascribed to the stability of the forces of nature, but to the will of God, who has charged the whole of his creation with his laws. "While the earth remains, seedtime and harvest, cold and heat, summer and winter, day and night, shall not cease" (Gen. 8:22). God's laws have determined the course of the stars (Ps. 148:6; Jer. 31:35) and fixed the elements: the sea (Job 38:10), the heavens (Job 38:33) and the earth (Jer. 33:25). All this was done so that the earth would be a suitable abode for man. This is also the meaning of the cosmic covenant which God concluded with Noah and his posterity after the flood: "When I bring clouds over the earth and the bow is seen in the clouds, I will remember my covenant, which is between me and you and every living creature of all flesh, and the waters shall never again become a flood to destroy all flesh. When the bow is in the clouds, I will look upon it and remember the everlasting covenant between God and every living creature of all flesh, that is upon the earth" (Gen. 9:14-16).

Are there then no limits to God's infinite power? What exists is surely not the result of his whim. Through the laws he imposed upon his creation an ordered and controlled existence was made possible for man and cosmos. Israel therefore accepted this cosmic order as a symbol of God's loyalty to his people and as an appeal on his part that they be mindful of him (Jer. 5:24; 8:7; 31:36). God's will is no momentary arbitrariness; it is determined through stability. Thus the Bible gives a different response than does science to the question about the origin of order in nature. While science looks for intrinsic earthy causes which shape this order, Scripture points above it to God, who gives meaning to this order. This different response arises from a fundamentally different consideration of reality. For science, "nature," as the reality with which it deals is called, is an objective datum to be considered — in se — and in such a way that no personal viewpoints have precedence over it. Everything one demands and finds originates within this space and does not go beyond it. The Biblical viewpoint is entirely different. For Scripture the world does not have this character of "nature" — of a datum that just happens to be. It could just as well not be. It is because God wills it to be; there is but one explanation: because God willed it.

The regularity of the natural event is from God, as is nature itself; hence no contradiction can arise within God's action, as if the natural order would be infringed upon and dislocated when God performs a miracle. The law of nature is not a hostile front that must be pierced, not a counterforce to be overpowered. Although nature, distinct from God, possesses a substantiality of its own, it has no independent grandeur but lies wholly in God's hand, as moldable clay in the hands of the potter. The distinction between what nature of itself can or can not do is pointless. What is important is that God can direct the laws of nature at any given moment to any specific purpose. From the viewpoint of nature, the difference between ordinary and extraordinary has little meaning; all events are, in the same way, God's works (Ps. 77:12; 86:8). Because "nature" is not mentioned in the Bible, the Psalms and Wisdom literature especially characterize the course of nature itself as miraculous (Ps. 89:6; 106:2; 139:14; Job 5:9). This does not alter the fact that this expression refers especially to divine power manifesting itself as a superior force in extraordinary events. It is shown in the very terminology which describes the miracle. God's power is experienced as "wonder"-ful when it is, for man, mysterious, strange, awe-inspiring, striking or brilliant. Thus God's activity is shaded in a multitude of words which now indicate greatness, now the astounding or terrifying side of his action. The magnitude of the Biblical way of thinking is that God reveals himself in extraordinary as well as in ordinary events; the Lord of nature is not only he who once created the world, but he who is continually active in it. Because the ordinary becomes routine and has no great impact on consciousness, the extraordinary happens now and then to draw man's attention again to the fact that he must see the invisible presence in the visible facts; and this presence leads everything in the direction he wills. Thus we are led from miracle as nature-event to its sign function and to the fact that miracles take place for the sake of man.

b. Miracles and history

When we establish that a miracle takes place for the sake of man we touch upon another important aspect. The miracle is not an occurrence taking place exclusively in nature's domain; it also belongs essentially within the domain of history. It exists only in connection with man and with God's activity for him. It is not an isolated phenomenon which we are unable to fit in place because it is exceptional; it is a link which has a complimentary function in the whole. God is, for Israel, not only the Lord of nature but also the Lord of history. This should really be expressed with much greater finesse. Israel discovered Yahweh as Lord of nature and Creator of the world only after realizing that he is the Lord not only of his own operations but of all universal events. From this Israel deduced that nature, as the workshop of history, has its origin in this one and same power. For Israel, the very creation of the world already belongs to the order of history. This creation is not a condition which gives history its

opening; it is the first salutary act of God in such
way that the genesis of the world and all that happens
in it are part of the history of salvation. We read
in Jeremiah the Prophet: "Thus says the Lord, the
God of Israel; it is I who by my great power and
my outstretched arm have made the earth, with the
men and animals that are on the earth, and I give
it to whomever it seems right to me. Now I have
given all these lands into the hand of Nebuchodono-
sor, the King of Babylon, my servant, and I have
given him also the beasts of the field to serve him.
All the nations shall serve him and his son and his
grandson, until the time of his own land comes;
then many nations and great kings shall make him
their slave" (Jer. 27:5-7). The same pattern is followed
in the description of how Israel shall be abandoned,
go into exile until it pleases God to allow his people
to return. Israel's faith in God did not develop from
theoretical speculations concerning God's power; it
has its basis in the conviction and experience of
God's presence and saving activity in history. This
arose from events which Israel experienced personally. Israel's history is, in a sense, the canvas on
which God's image is painted.[3] This faith-conviction
leads Israel back to the unforgettable experience of
the exodus from Egypt and the passage through
the Red Sea, the wandering through the desert and
the entry into the Promised Land. Israel then experienced God's intervention with such an intensity
that it stamped these events as miracles. The char-
acterization of these facts as miracles does not come
about by means of a scientific critique of the laws

of nature but rests upon an experience of what is normal in history. The miracle is something extraordinary because God manifests himself in it as a God who saves. The miracle-event thus becomes a sign which points like a finger to the always-near and all-directing God. This is in contrast to the everyday routine events behind which he is hidden from us.

c. Miracles as God's revelation of salvation

In order to understand any fact as a sign, an intuitive comprehension is required; to be able to see this phenomenon as a sign of salvation, a salvation-consciousness is demanded. This means that certain historical facts — and miracles as well — can then only be understood as a salvation event through adjusted listening and correct interpretation. Only through salvific experience is Israel able to see its history as God's activity for his people. His revelation becomes known as a divine operation only after what happens in nature and history is prophetically interpreted.[4] A prophet is a man who, by virtue of divine calling "knows" with God — the man who views God's historical work with him. It is therefore not accidental that along with the cardinal events which happen in Israel, and which bear the miracle-character through being God-filled, the prophet too appears on the stage as one who, by divine direction, is possessed of more than ordinary stature. It is he who through his prophetic experience defines the religious element and consequently the religious meaning of the natural phenomenon. We may ascribe

the passage through the Red Sea to a strong east
wind, which God made blow. We must, however,
bear in mind that this purely physical fact could
never have acquired the character of a miracle if it
had not been interpreted as such by God's prophet.
Interpretation is inseparably connected with physical
events.

Prophetic interpretation creates the religious facts
— creates the miracle. Let this be distinctly understood: for a competent observer, the whole of nature
constantly manifests the wondrous activity of God.
This too is the starting point for the prophet. But
in certain circumstances of place and time, this is
intensified by the prophet and given a new perspective when incorporated into a distinct historical context. From the historical writings of Israel it thus
becomes clear that the Bible is not as concerned with
history as such as it is with God's activity in history.
Hence Israel looks upon history as a history of salvation, namely, as a self-unfolding revelation of
persons or facts. Is there then still room here for
historical authenticity? By all means — yes! As long
as this does not mean: it happened exactly as related
here. It is necessary that the facts, at least in sub-
stance, are in accord with the real course of things.
Genuine reality must be the basis of religious, prophetic interpretation. This reality will manifest the
meaning which God conveys through the actual fact.

A striking illustration of this is, for instance, the
Elias and Eliseus accounts, a separate collection in
the Book of Kings. No one will deny that these

accounts are embellished with legendary elements.
They vie to give both men the same prophetic stature.
Hence the different parallel accounts. The Eliseus
cycle is especially unable to restrain itself regarding
the miraculous. The Elias figure is notably restrained,
and this is the intention of the author. The main
feature is the struggle for pure Yahwism at a time
when Israel's dynasty of kings led the way in the
service of Baal, and practiced the fertility cult which
came from Tyre. The focus of attention in this
critical time for Yahwism is on Elias and Eliseus.
Elias' contribution to the struggle wins over Eliseus'
by far. The victory of Yahwism over the Baal wor-
ship is personified in him. It goes without saying that
the event on Mount Carmel must be interpreted in
this sense (1 Kings 18). It is needless to ask what
an impersonal and disinterested spectator-scientist
would have thought. What is of interest is the fact
that Israel, in the person of Elias, overcame a religious crisis and thereby found the correct interpretation — the relationship of God with nature. Moreover, the after-effects of his struggle for Yahweh
were so strong that his stature has been compared
with that of Moses. This cycle of accounts demon-
strates clearly that although the purely historical
nucleus of facts is almost impossible to ascertain, the
prophetic interpretation accurately pointed out the
essence of the event.

d. The composition of the miracle-event through Israel's theological reflection

As Israel becomes more intensely conscious of its

religious dimensions it deepens its notions of history as salvific history. From this more profound stance it begins to realize new facts in a deeper perspective; events of the past are again scrutinized and, if need be, once more and differently interpreted. This re-interpretation obviously produces a new perspective of the facts. It reduces to this: divine intervention is extremely accentuated. This is brought about by leaving out, or casting into the shadow, created causes, thereby presenting the intervention of God as miraculous and spectacular. A spiritualized inter-pretation of the fact is presented. Let us look at this more closely.

The same Scriptural immediacy applies to God's direction in history as applies to his activity in crea-tion. Omission of intermediate causes accentuates the fact that God is the Lord who does all. An illuminating example of this neglect of the inter-position of natural causes to show the divine activity to better advantage is 2 Kings 19:35-37. Here we are told that Yahweh's angel, in the camp of the Assyrians besieging Jerusalem, strikes down 185,000 men to save the holy city. The hagiographer points to the salvific-historical meaning of the catastrophe. The actual question as to what the natural cause (prob-ably pestilence) might have been lies outside the author's purpose.

"This interpretation" says Guardini, "resembles the one we find on old inscriptions where the ruler says: 'In the year so and so, have I conquered so and so many people, built such and such cities,

provided stores etc.' The acting generals and officials
have disappeared: the ruler alone is mentioned."⁵

That Israel manifests little interest in an exact
description of the wondrous facts as supernatural
phenomena can be illustrated with the development
which any given theme underwent in the course of
its tradition. To impress the religious-historical character of the primeval events surrounding the origins
of Israel upon later generations, the Israelitic tradition took some liberties. This finds expression in
the way the effect of God's power is highlighted.
We offer some data to illustrate this. The superiority
of Yahweh's power over Egyptian sorcery is described
in the plagues of Egypt; this is a narrative in which
the Judaic authors could not resist accentuating the
wondrous character of the plagues. There is no
doubt that they relished doing this. The plague itself
is a typically Egyptian natural phenomenon; it
occurred generally in the East, at times was common
to Palestine. The prose narrative is found in Ex.
7:14-21, 41. The poetic form is in Ps. 78:43-51 and
105:28-36, while Wisd. 11:6-20 and 16-18 gives
entirely its own adaptation of the facts. In the epic
narrative itself divers traditions marking the stages
of its growth are already present. One mentions
six or seven plagues, another four or five. Partial
overlapping occurs. The number grows. Swift suc-.
cession and catastrophic effect of the plagues suggest divine intervention. The climax of the narrative
is, without doubt, the paschal night with the death
of Egypt's sons.

Another significant example is the passage through
the Red Sea.[6] It is part of the Judaic creed that
Yahweh led his people from Egypt with a mighty
hand, through great terror, with signs and wonders
(Deut. 26:8). Protection from Egypt's pursuing army
is one of those miracles. "Then I brought your
fathers out of Egypt, and you came to the sea; and
the Egyptians pursued your fathers with chariots and
horsemen to the Red Sea. And when they cried to
the Lord, he put darkness between you and the
Egyptians, and made the sea come upon them and
cover" (Josh. 24:6). This fact offered ample oppor-
tunity for successful, popular embroidery and, at the
same time, for theological interpretation. From the
beginning, different wondrous facts are connected.
They highlight the desperate position of Israel, thus
making Yahweh's show of power shine even more
brilliantly. The camp was positioned at a place which
makes hope of escape impossible and promptly en-
tices Pharaoh to press his pursuit (Ex. 14:1-10). Emphasis is put on the superior power of his army
(14:6), on the panic among Israel's sons (14:10) and
on the resolute attitude of Moses, who assures the
people of Yahweh's help (14:13). Then the cloud
is placed between the Israelites and the enemy's
army. Yahweh throws back the sea by means of a
strong east wind. He routes the army of the Egyptians (according to Ps. 76:17-19 by a thunderstorm),
clogging the wheels of the chariots, and at this
critical moment the sea returns to its wonted flow.
Israel is saved (14:19-31). Tradition has particularly
exploited the moment of the passage itself.

The first version is fairly scanty: "Then Moses stretched out his hand over the sea; and Yahweh drove the sea back with a strong east wind all night" (Ex. 14: 21). The other version shows a preference for detail and a leaning toward the miraculous: "Yahweh made the sea dry land and the waters were divided. And the people of Israel went into the midst of the sea on dry ground, the waters being a wall to them on their right hand and on their left" (Ex. 14:21-22). To this, Wisd. 19:7 adds: "Dry land appeared, where water was before, and in the Red Sea always without hindrance and out of the great deep in a springing field." In the end there is no sea to be seen: "The sea looked and fled" (Ps. 114:3). We observe development from the strong east wind making the sea fordable, to rising walls of water to an ever-extending dry land.

We find this same evolution in the narrative of water coming from the rock (Ex. 17:6): "And you shall strike the rock, and water shall come out of it, that the people may drink. And Moses did so in the sight of the elders of Israel" (cf. Num. 20:11). Ps. 105:41: "He opened the rock, and the water gushed forth; it flowed through the desert like a river." Ps. 114:8: "(Yahweh), who turns the rock into a pool of water, the flint into a spring of water." The striking of the rock is exaggerated into a splitting. The riches of water swell to a stream that flows through the desert; the rock becomes a pool. It is theologically important that these excessive baroque embellishments in the presentation of the facts are not depicted for the sake of the miraculous; they intend to demonstrate, above all, that just as creation

came forth from God's omnipotent will, so Israel,
through the same free creative power, was made
into a people — it owes its election to this. A composition of another sort lies in an idealized interpretation of the fact, which at the same time mag-
nifies Israel's guilt.[7]

According to Jer. 2:1-3 and Hos. 13:4-5 the journey
through the desert was the occasion of a mutually
beneficial relationship between Yahweh and Israel.
It was the honeymoon of the people. Israel belonged
totally to Yahweh, and had not yet given itself over to
idolatry. The people were dependent on Yahweh
for everything and he took care of everything. This
care, with the accompanying self-surrender of Israel,
finds expression in the description of the miracle of
the manna. This is the bread God gives Israel to
eat; it rains from heaven (Ex. 16:4). Here is the
description of the miracle: "And in the morning, dew
lay round about the camp. And when the dew
had gone up, there was on the face of the wilderness
a fine, flakelike thing, fine as hoar-frost on the ground.
When the people of Israel saw it they said to one
another What it is? for they did not know what it
was. And Moses said to them, It is the bread which
the Lord has given you to eat" (Ex. 16:13-15).
Everyone gathers, no one is deprived. God gives each
what he needs. Confidence in this demands that
they daily rely on him. No one is allowed to store
it except on the day before the Sabbath. Besides,
it does not keep. Those who try to hoard find it
decayed the next day. Israel enjoys this favor until
she reaches the frontiers of Canaan (Ex. 16:16-36).

In Psalm 78:25 this bread which rained from heaven becomes heavenly bread: "Men ate of the bread of the angels." Although another tradition mentions that Israel criticized this manna in the end (Num. 11:5), Wisd. 16:20 says: "Thou didst feed thy people with the food of angels and gavest them bread from heaven, having in it all that is delicious, and the sweetness of every taste."

The bread, at first only the origin of which is reported (bread from heaven), later is substantially described (heavenly bread, bread of the angels), and in the end it is endowed with still more qualities. In Deut. 8:3 a paradigm is added: Israel should have learned from this that they live not only by earthly food but by all that comes from the mouth of God.

The opposite of this miracle-rich time is the question as to how Israel behaved. Presentation of this is increasingly negative (Ps. 78; 106; Ezek. 20). Some ancient traditions mentioned the grumbling of Israel on several occasions. According to the prophets, the time in the desert is a time of trial, a challenge from Yahweh. In Ezekiel this leads to a threat: as the fathers in the desert were judged, so God will bring Israel into the wilderness of the nations to undergo his judgment (Ezek. 20:35).

But in this abandonment the faith of the prophets is not shaken. In this darkness the luminous word is spoken that Yahweh will once more redeem Israel and lead his people through the desert. Israel clings to this expectation unfalteringly (Is. 43:16-21; 48:20;

52:12). This is not without reason. A miracle brings
man into contact with a reality of a different order;
he feels infallibly that it plays an important part in
his life. He feels even more — his very existence is
at stake.

e.   Miracles as a sign and pledge of salvation

What reaction does a miracle produce in man?[8]
For him who experiences it in its true dimensions it
becomes clear that the unusualness of the perceptible
event is meant to manifest more than it is capable
of expressing in itself. In other words, the uncom-
monness of the phenomenon suggests something of
a higher and more spiritual order which can usually
be made known to man only in this way. The sign
signifies no more nor less than that man experiences
God as present and active, and precisely so in this
event. Man through this experience comes under the
influence of a reality different from the one he
draws from himself. Thus he finds himself within
the ambit of God's presence, where he experiences
God as the Omnipotent One who has no limits, as
the Indenpendent One who is responsible only to
himself, as the Holy One who can say "I am." He
here touches a reality which makes him feel that he
could not exist before and in this reality, had God
not given him the grace. The miracle enters the life
of man as an "appearance" of God; at the same time
it illuminates his own being. It shows him what he
is — a dependent, miserable, sinful man. Peter, after
the miracle of the fishes, reacted perfectly when he
cried out: "Go from me Lord, for I am a sinful man."

It is an echo of the cry of the prophet Isaias, when he beheld God in a vision: "Woe is me, for I am lost, for my eyes have seen the King, the Lord of Hosts" (Is. 6:5).

A miracle is not without danger for man. It certainly is not a mere sensation, nor does it serve as gratification of curiosity. One whom a miracle touches is cured of all desire for it. The real miracle stirs man, either as a support for his trust in God, or as an appeal to better his ways, or as a call to fulfill a mission. This contact by way of warning leads the responsive man beyond every possible rational speculation and advice offered in defense; it leads him to believe in God's dominion over his life, to bend toward this and to expect a future in the other world: that which announced itself on this natural plane will become his one day. This faith in God's providence now, and this expectation of the future is a fundamental thought which permeates Israel's life. Both find their support in God's miracles. God's intervention in Israel was never more grandiose than at the time of Israel's origin. Nowhere is it so clear that Yahweh is the powerful and considerate Shepherd who walks before and leads his flock. Here is one of those concrete, historical events, through which the idea of Yahweh's Kingship came into being; here is one of those striking victories over the enemy and wondrous delivery from distress through which Yahweh's superiority becomes visible. An old victory-song thus interprets this: "Who is like Thee, O Lord, among the gods. Who is like Thee, majestic in holiness, terrible in glorious deeds, doing wonders? Thou didst stretch out thy right hand, the earth swallowed them. Thou hast led in thy steadfast love the people whom thou hast redeemed, thou hast guided them by thy strength to thy holy abode" (Ex. 15:11-13).

And the final chord: "The Lord will reign for ever and ever" (vs. 18). God's kingship, which sounds in the Exodus song, is connected with his providential care and guidance. Therefore the admonition which runs through the whole of Israel's history is to remember that period of grace with which God began his reign over Israel.[9]

This reign of God finds an earthly setback in David's kingship. The full flowering of his reign is withheld by the infidelity of Israel during the period of the Kings after David; the purpose of this reign was not fully realized under David and Solomon. Expectation arises that God will establish his final reign through a new Anointed One from the House of David. This reign will be so complete that there will be no power except the God on whom everything depends. All God's enemies will be slain; Israel itself will be cleansed of its sins by God and sanctified anew. Then the acceptable time of justice, love and lasting peace will dawn. This is the time of which Jeremiah writes: "Behold, the days are coming, says the Lord, when I will make a new covenant with the house of Israel and the house of Judah . . . . for I will forgive their iniquity, and I will remember their sins no more" (Jer. 31:31-34).

The Book of Isaias too, sings of the new time which God will begin in the end; this is coupled with remission of sins (Is. 43:25), will abolish human suffering and reinstate the state of paradise: "He will come and save you! Then the eyes of the blind shall be opened and the ears of the deaf unstopped; then shall the lame man leap like a hart, and the tongue of the dumb sing for joy" (Is. 35:5-6).

Here an idea which plays an important part in Israel's expectation comes to the fore: the last days will be like the beginning; in the end the primordial age returns. So the notion is gradually established, that God's guidance shall reach its goal only when such a wondrous intervention again takes place, as when Israel passed through the sea. The Messianic time is often painted by the prophets in pictures drawn from the delivery from Egypt; but one knows positively that the coming deliverance from anxiety and infidelity by far surpasses the first.

Hence the true exodus still lies in the future. This concerns not only Israel but all nations. The election and redemption connected with the first exodus are the central salvific events in which the mystery of God's dealing with the whole world is to be understood. By the original exodus Israel was designated one day to become the central point of a world where all nations shall belong to God. In this way Yahweh's reign as King spreads over the whole world. This is not to be understood as if Yahweh were not king over the whole world from the beginning. No;

he manifests his kingship from the time of creation;
therefore he can again and again intervene victorious-
ly to reveal and confirm this kingship. That which he
began in the creation he continues in history. As
God once chained the powers of chaos, so he confirms his act of creation in history by repeatedly
shackling threatening world powers. Since God was
in the beginning, so he shall also be in the end. In
other words, the powers may triumph temporarily
but they shall eventually perish. That is the prospect
of a final revelation of God's reign as King. What is
posed in the creation as principle shall, through
the struggle of the ages, come to perfect realization.
Therefore, every intervention of God in history is
at the same time a confirmation of his act of creation
and a pledge of his coming final victory. Thus a
miracle can be understood only in connection with
creation and eschatology. What takes place in the
miracle is this: it effects that the new heaven and
the new world project their luster into the present;
it makes known the fact that God designedly permits
his power to be experienced in an anticipatory way,
and that earthly redemption and restoration from
human misery are but a first step toward coming
spiritual salvation. The miracle is an "epiphany"; it
is the appearance pointing to another reality, a signal
to remind us of it. Therefore, he who has gone
adrift within this world is not able to grasp the
meaning of a miracle. For him it is a scandal and
annoyance. This dark side of miracles is very clearly
accentuated in the New Testament. Christ himself
becomes a sign of contradiction.

2

MIRACLES AND THE
PROCLAMATION OF GOD'S
DOMINION IN THE NEW TESTAMENT

1. Irrefutable facts

The testimony of the New Testament proves beyond all doubt that **Jesus** fulfilled his mission, given by God, in power of word and deed.[10] Since the very origin of the Church, his miracles therefore form a very important part of the apostolic preaching. In the first discourse of Peter with the gathered crowd at Pentecost, we read: "Men of Israel, hear these words: Jesus of Nazareth, a man attested to you by God with mighty works and wonders and signs, which God did through him in your midst, as you yourselves know" (Acts 2:22). On a later occasion: "You know the word which was proclaimed throughout all Judea, beginning from Galilee after the baptism which John preached: how God anointed Jesus of Nazareth with the Holy Spirit and with power: how he went about doing good and healing all that were oppressed by the devil, for God was with him" (Acts 10:37-38).

All documents in which the apostolic preaching of the Gospel is verified unanimously state that Jesus

healed the sick, raised the dead, freed the possessed
from demons and commanded nature. Some twenty
texts in the Gospels mention that he performed many
miracles. In addition, a number of exactly described
cases is preserved. In one or other, possibly, there is
a question of repetition; this is of little moment in
view of the great number of recorded facts. Even
the critical man of today who finds it difficult to
accept the possibility and reality of a miracle cannot
and may not ignore these reports without conscien-
tious inquiry. Beacons to keep his bearings and
stay in a safe channel are found both in and outside
Scripture.

The miracle stories take up such a prominent place
in the Gospels that without them little or nothing
would remain. This is very clear in Mark's Gospel.
In contrast to Matthew, Mark mentions few great
addresses. Jesus' preaching is interlarded between
the miracle narratives. With the other evangelists
as well, these miracle records are not just casually
inserted embellishments which one could eliminate
from the Gospels without damage; they are elements
which essentially contribute to the gospel structure.
The belief and unbelief of Jesus' disciples, the fear
and astonishment of the people, the hatred of his
antagonists and the confusion of their conduct is,
without these miracles, absolutely unthinkable. That
Jesus' antagonists never denied the actuality of his
deeds is also important. To their discomfort, they
had to agree: he performs miracles, he casts out
devils; but spitting their gall they added "by the

power of satan" (Mk. 3:22). According to John 11:47,
Jesus is arrested as a seducer of the people because
of his miracles.

In the later rabbinic-Judaic polemics against Christ
and Christianity, Jesus' miracles remain in the fore-
ground. His deeds serve to accuse him of magic
and tricks of the devil and are used as the motive
for his condemnation as a seducer of the people and
a false prophet.

The miracles of the Gospel are often belittled from
a religious-psychological point of view with the alle-
gation that, in religious circles, miracle stories are
believed only too eagerly, and are consequently accepted without any criticism; or what is worse, their
effects are magnified and their number increased.
But then, Jesus' antagonists too were hostile, hyper-
critical and captious. They demanded other signs
from him, and fanatically argued about his miracles
(Jn. 10:21); their misconceptions underline their
rancor. But they were not so blind that they became
excited about something which did not take place.
The objection is no longer valid, that all religious
personalities are encircled with a miracle-halo and
that therefore the Gospel narratives are purposely
biased. Facts do not agree with this. In the New
Testament itself, the Baptist ranks as the greatest
personality before Christ: "I tell you, among those
born of woman, none is greater than John" (Lk. 7:28);
but no miracles are attributed to him: "And many
came to him; and they said; John did no sign, but
everything that John said about this man is true"

(Jn. 10:41). This is so true that even in circles where
Jesus is considered the satanic opponent of John,
the salvation-figure, miracles are attributed to him
and not to John.

Something similar strikes us in the old Islamic
literature. As a prophet and miracle worker Jesus
is highly rated, but not nearly as high as Mohammed,
who lacks miracle powers. Religious-historical comparison compels the Gospel story to be taken seriously. Miracles contrast sharply with the various
sorceries, pseudo-miracles and magic deeds so frequently and enthusiastically described in contem-
porary writings. By contrast with these absurdities,
common to the imaginative miracle stories of post-
Apostolic times, the Gospel descriptions of miracles
present an image of authenticity. However, important though this principal insight into the historical
trustworthiness of the Gospel miracle-narratives
might be, it is still obvious that the "wonder"ful
aspect of miracles is not thereby resolved. It remains
possible to deny miracles or to remain indifferent.
Many people ignored the miracles of Christ or were
unimpressed by them; his enemies would not accept
them. For this reason, contradiction belongs to
miracles as shadow to light.

Miracles are not restricted to Jesus alone in the
New Testament. He gives power to his disciples
during his public life to drive out unclean spirits and
to heal diseases and maladies (Mt. 10:1). Shortly
before he leaves this world, he predicts signs and
miracles which will accompany all who believe (Mk.

16:17). The miracle in the young Christian community is a fact that speaks for itself. Of the many miracles and signs performed by the Apostles (Acts 2:43; 5:12), the healing of the lame man is mentioned in detail because this causes the first conflict with the synagogue (Acts, Chapters 3 and 4). Emphasis is given to the name of Jesus (3:6; 3:16; 4:12; 4:30) through which the healing takes place. This serves to emphasize that the gift of performing miracles does not belong to the community itself but is a power delegated by God.

The Apostles in Jerusalem and the deacon, Stephen, "full of grace and power, did great wonders and signs among the people" (Acts 6:8). In Samaria, where the deacon Philip preached the Christ, ". . . the multitudes with one accord gave heed to what was said by Philip, when they heard him and saw the signs, which he did. For unclean spirits came out of many who were possessed, and many who were lame or paralyzed were healed. So there was much joy in that city" (8:6-8). In all the vicissitudes of their apostolic journeys, Paul and Barnabas had confidence in the Lord, "Who bore witness to the word of his grace, granting signs and wonders to be done by their hands" (14:3); and this happened not only among the Jews, but also among the gentiles. After Peter had argued for reception of the gentiles into the Church without the encumbrance of the Jewish law, "they listened to Barnabas and Paul as they related what signs and wonders God had done through them among the gentiles" (Acts 15:12). More

references to miracles can be found in Acts 13:6-12;
16:18; 19:12-20; 20:7-12; 28:3-10.

The epistles of Paul consider it normal that
wonders and signs accompany and confirm the
preaching of the Gospel. In a summarized remark
to the congregation in Rome, Paul writes that the
Lord has through him (Paul) been at work "by the
power of signs and wonders, by the power of the
Holy Spirit" (Rom. 15:19). The gift of performing
miracles is, for him, a testimonial of his authentic
office of apostle; "For I am not at all inferior to
these superlative apostles, even though I am nothing.
The signs of a true apostle were performed among
you in all patience, with signs and wonders and
mighty works" (2 Cor. 12:12). The Epistle to the
Hebrews, too, mentions the power to perform miracles given to the apostles: "For if the message declared by angels was valid and every transgression
or disobedience received a just retribution, how shall
we escape if we neglect such a great salvation? It
was declared at first by the Lord and it was attested
to us by those who heard him, while God also bore
signs and wonders and various miracles, and by the
gifts of the Holy Spirit distributed according to his
own will" (Heb. 2:2-4). This operation of the Spirit
is not restricted to the apostles. In a catalogue of
the gifts of grace received by the Church of Corinth,
the power of signs and wonders is mentioned again
as an operation of the Spirit (1 Cor. 12:9-10) and the
gift is highly rated; they who possess it are mentioned
among the great functionaries in the Church; the

apostles, the prophets and the teachers etc. (1 Cor. 12:28-30).

In summary: New Testament writings unanimously assert that the power to perform miracles is not limited to the time of Jesus' public life; this gift remains active in the Church. It becomes clear however that it is not given to every Christian to perform miracles (1 Cor. 10:29). It is bestowed on those who are inspired by the Spirit in a special manner: the apostles and prophets and those whom the Spirit chooses according to his will. We too must emphasize that the miracle is not just a confirmation and a sanction of the office, but an essential emolument for the preaching of the Gospel, which has for its object faith in the saving revelation of God's power.

2. In search of the meaning

Why are miracles mentioned in the Gospels? What inspired the first preachers of the faith when they spoke and illustrated the facts? Why were the miracle narratives so important in their eyes? A valuable indication is produced by semantics. The Evangelists use three different words: they speak of "wonders," of "powers" and of "signs." It is surely noteworthy that the word "miracle" is never mentioned without one or both of the others. It would seem that the evangelists wish to see in e.g. a healing by Jesus more than just an extraordinary event, a surprising deviation from the ordinary course of things. Naturally, the first thing which comes to our

attention in Christ's miracles is the exceptional case
— sudden cure of incurable disease, raising from the
dead, etc., evoke the surprise of the eye-witnesses
(Mk. 5:42; Lk. 7:16). This proves that they are not
interested in Jesus as a miracle-worker in the sense
of the Hellenic wonder stories, which stress the
bizarre, grotesque, disproportionate and mysterio-
magical that it inevitably leads to the glorification
of the person of the performer. If the writers had
any intention of giving Jesus the reputation of
wonder-worker, as was the case in the above-
mentioned literature, they should then have added a
good deal more baroque and embroidery to their
miracle descriptions.

The Scriptural accent, however, is on power manifestation and on the sign. In this the Gospels con-
tinue the genuine concepts of the Old Testament.
But the new trend lies in this, that the miracle as
power expression and sign points fully to the central
mystery of the Gospel: the mystery of the Person of
the Lord. Manifestation of this is the meaning of
Jesus' miracles.

To see them solely or chiefly as signs of the Lord's
pity for the suffering and infirm is to underestimate
their worth. It is true that the Evangelists tell us
that the Lord has pity (Mk. 6:34; 8:2; Mt. 9:36; 14:14;
15:32; 20:34), but in most cases it is not mentioned.
The reason is that miracles seemingly do not have
as their object the revelation of subjective motives,
attitudes or reactions of the Lord. The Gospel, as a
whole does not allow this compassion to be under-

stood as the tenderness of one who cannot see another
suffer. His miracles are, therefore, no **pièces
d'occasion** of mercy, performed from motives of compassion, in response to an urge to alleviate a pressing
immediate need. Nor are they an expression of a
feeling of solidarity with the socially weakest faction.

Miracles are not recorded to present Jesus psy-
chologically; they are narrated to express his
redemptive-historical value. The miracle does reveal
"the humanity and charity of God, our Redeemer"
(Tit. 3:4); it is a sign of the Redemption, bringing
goodness and presence of God in Jesus: "A great
prophet has arisen among us and God has visited
his people" (Lk. 7:16). Miracles are meant to give
us a view of the heart of the God who loves us.
Jesus was not concerned with man because of his
human compassion; this obviously is present in him
in highest degree. He was especially indignant about
the damage caused by the power of the evil one.
Behind the leper, the possessed, the dead, Jesus per-
ceives the enemy. Characteristic, therefore, is the
double interpretation of the healing of the leper
(Mk. 1:41): "Jesus moved with pity, stretched out
his hand," or "Jesus, grim and angry stretched out
his hand." Both belong together; compassion for a
man tied down and wrath at the destroying power
— a compassion and wrath which moves Jesus to
tears (Jn. 11:33-38).

To reveal the charity and mercy of God is **one** of
the meanings of a miracle. It does point to the
person of the Redeemer; but it also points to its

effect, the Redemption. It is an act of power by which God's opponent is repulsed. It is a breakthrough of the divine into this world and at the same time a sign of this divine world. Seen from Jesus' consciousness of mission and power, miracles are called works or powers; for those upon whom or before whose eyes they are performed, they are also signs which perceptibly announce what God wants to say to man. They are God speaking in an unmistakable language and are already a visible interpretation of what God pronounces in this message: redemption from sin and death, the never-to-be-lost splendor of human life. The purpose of the miracle is none other than that God himself willed to become man for us, to choose the cross and to rise in bodily glory.

When it is said that the purpose of miracles is to prove the divine mission of Christ, this, properly understood, is perfectly correct. But in the explanation it must be made clear that the miracle has an extrinsic connection with Jesus' message as a power expression which authenticates his mission from outside; the miracle itself intrinsically forms part of his mission and commission, and is its realization. Miracles themselves are gospel, glad tidings indeed. In other words the miracle legitimates Christ's message and heralds the world to come. This demands further development.

3. Miracles — breakthrough of the coming world
a. Christ, the power of God (1 Cor. 1:24)

The Old Testament concept that God reveals him-

self in creation and history mainly through his power
is consistently continued in the New. The power
of God is so identified with God's being, that Jesus
could say before the Sanhedrin: ". . . and you will
see the Son of Man sitting at the right hand of
power" (Mk. 14:62; Mt. 26:64). This attribute, referred
to throughout the New Testament, is in essence related to the Spirit of God, (Lk. 1:17-35; 4:14; Acts
1:8), to the Kingdom of God (Mk. 9:1; Mt. 6:13),
to the grace of God (Acts 6:8; Eph. 3:7), to the glory
of God (Mk. 13:26; Eph. 1:18; Col. 1:11) — and to
the miracles which themselves are called powers.
It is striking that the New Testament constantly
speaks of a veiling of this power and this prefers
to operate in the infirmity of human existence or,
as in Paul's version, in the infirmity of human
service '(2 Cor. 2:1-10).

The main point of the whole theme of Mark's
gospel is to show that during his lifetime Christ was
the hidden Son of Man and that only through his
resurrection did he become the Son of Man in power
and majesty. Jesus himself is God incognito. Hence
the contrast between the weakness of the flesh which
he inhabited and the power of the resurrection:
"Who was decended from David according to the
flesh and designated Son of God in power according
to the Spirit of holiness by his resurrection from
the dead" (Rom. 1:4; 2 Cor. 13:4; Phil. 2:7).

The same can be said of the mystery of God's
dominion. This is manifest only in faith although

it is in reality present and efficacious in this world.
The Kingdom is like yeast invisibly mixed with flour
(Mt. 13:33), a precious pearl hidden in a field (Mt.
13:44, seed sprouting in dark secrecy (Mk. 4:26-29).
It is therefore possible to overlook it, or to con-
sciously ignore it. To know the mysteries of the
Kingdom of God is given only to Jesus' diciples (Mk.
4:11-12). Christ thanks his Father that he has hidden
the mysteries of the Kingdom from the wise and
understanding, and revealed them to babes (his
disciples) (Mt. 11:25).

Although the Evangelists, each in his own way,
insist on this mystery, at the same time they stress
that God's power acts in Christ and that this is manifested in the miracle narratives. Healing follows an
authoritative word, a resolution of the will. Jesus
drives out devils with the command "Be silent and
come out of him" (Mk. 1:25; cf. 5:8 and 9:25). He
stills the storm by the power of his word (Mk. 4:39).
With a word he heals a blind man (Mk. 10:52), a
withered hand (Mk. 3:5), a leper (Mk. 1:40; cf. Mt.
8:1-4).

Naturally, in performing a miracle actions and
gestures are used: Christ stretches out his hand and
touches the sick man (Mk. 1:41). He touches the
part to be healed (Mk. 7:32; Mt. 9:29) and makes use
of spittle and mud (Mk. 7:33; 8:23). This is not
concerned with healing techniques or magical manip-
ulations; it serves to illustrate what he says and does,
and sometimes has a symbolic meaning. The healing does not take place through the gesture but

through the word. The power of Jesus' word reveals his participation with the creative power of God's word, through which the world came into being and remains preserved (Gen. 1:3, 6, 9; Ps. 33:6, 9; 147:18). Christ's work acquires the character of a new creation. The exclamation of the onlookers after the healing of the deaf and dumb man, "He has done all things well" (Mk. 7:37) may be considered a recollection of what was written after the creation of heaven and earth: "And God saw everything that he had made, and behold it was very good" (Gen. 1:31).

The New Testament aims to show Christ's power as equal to the Father's. This man, weak as he may be, can call his own what belongs to God alone. The word he speaks is nothing less than a presentation to men of the divine creative word which was at the beginning of all things. This man is present and active as is the living God himself. Come to this realization through faith, Peter cries out: "You are the Christ, the Son, of the living God" (Mt. 16:16). Christ is the power of God in action. He and the Father are one. "My Father is working still and I am working. The Son can do nothing of his own, but only what he sees the Father doing; for whatever he does, that the Son does likewise" (Jn. 5:17-19). With this Christ bears witness against the pharisees that the miracle performed by him on the Sabbath (Jn. 5:1-18) must be seen as a revelation of the saving power of the love of God who works in him. Not only this miracle, but all salvific human deeds of

Christ are thus the revelation of God to men. The divine salvation action translates itself continuously into the human deeds of the Lord. This is what is meant when Scripture speaks about the progressive breakthrough of the Kingdom of God, which takes place in and through the person of Jesus Christ. God's power which, according to the testimony of the Old Testament, is active in history and gives it form and propels it to a meaningful end, is present in the Christ-reality of the New Testament. Once and for all, in this (him) the active power of God is perfectly represented.

b. The driving out of devils and the presentation of the Kingdom

The most important part of Christ's preaching about the Kingdom of God does not consist of a totally new content which departs from the expectation of the Old Testament. Jesus began his preaching of the Kingdom without any introduction or explanation and without any reaction of misunderstanding from his audience. No, the novelty lies first of all in the announcement of the immediate proximity of this powerful intervention of God at the end time. The message is sensational in the warning cry: "The time is fulfilled and the Kingdom of God is at hand. Repent, and believe in the gospel" (Mk. 1:15). Like a relay runner, he has taken over this word of the Baptist to pass it on in turn to his disciples. But this cannot be the most important fact. If Jesus had been solely a prophet of this eschatological Kingdom, he would have been no more and would have done no more than the Baptist. Jesus is more and does more. He brings his own person into essential union with the divine dominion. There is an unbreakable relationship between him and the reality of the Kingdom itself. Scripture gives unmistakable indications of this. The inseparable parallel between the preaching and the salvific act is the best testimony. Jesus does not just announce; he brings something to realization; he effects what he announces. In his action he brings about the Kingdom of God.[11]

An important text which connects the works of Jesus directly with the depths of the dominion of God is the interpretation he gives to the casting out of devils (Mt. 12:25-37; Lk. 11:17-23; Mk. 3:22-30). The reaction of the people is positive: "Never was anything like this seen in Israel" (Mt. 9:33) and "Can this be the son of David?" (Mt. 12:23). The pharisees, however, consider him as suspect and vilify him: "It is only by Beelzebub, the prince of demons, that this man casts out demons" (Mt. 12:24), and still worse: "He is possessed by Beelzebub" (Mk. 3:22). Jesus conclusively refutes the absurdity of their imputations by indicating the overt contradiction between the two groups (Mk. 12:24, 29).

The hostile attitude in which the encounter takes place is sufficient proof. Collusion is out of the question. Communication is lacking. The demons shout at him like barking dogs (Mk. 1:23; 3:11; 5:7; 9:27). Jesus commands. The word he speaks is a command (Mk. 1:25; 1:27; 3:12; 9:25). He disposes of them; he cuts their protestations short, and casts them out immediately (Mk. 1:25; 5:8). Satan cannot, through Christ, cast out other demons without at the same time destroying his own hold on men and destroying himself. Because, "if satan has risen up against himself and is divided, he cannot stand, but is coming to an end" (Mk. 3:26).

Jesus does not merely defend himself in the controversy with the pharisees; he opens the attack. If the pharisees accuse him, have they ever stopped to think about the source from which their own exorcists draw their power? What can they respond to such an accusation? With condemnation: "Therefore they shall be your judges" (Mt. 12:27). Jesus' answer, begun as an argument containing both defense and attack, concludes with a solemn testimony on the origin of his power: it is the Spirit of God (like the finger of God) through whom I accomplish this. But then the conclusion too, is inevitable: "But if it is by the finger (the Spirit) of God that I cast out demons, then the Kingdom of God has come upon you" (Mt. 12:28; Lk. 11:20).

In the light of Jesus' self-consciousness this statement is extremely interesting. He is not only the more powerful one who conquered satan; through his struggle-obtained victory the dominion of God has come within reach of this world. The nearness and presence of this divine domination can be seen in the effective casting out of demons. In and through the power granted to Jesus the eschatological Kingdom obtains a footing. The different versions — "finger of God" and "Spirit of God" — appear in the

narrative of the plagues of Egypt (Ex. 8:15; 8:19).
The first two plagues were called forth through
Aaron's rod; they were imitated by the Egyptian
magicians. But with the third plague — the gnats —
the power of Egypt's magic ran aground. The
magicians recognized a higher force in Aaron's rod;
they capitulated to this greater prowess with the
cry: "This is the finger of God" (Ex. 8:19), this deed
is the work of a divine power.

By appealing to the "finger of God" as a reminder
(Ex. 8:15), Christ's actions insist on the presence of
divine superiority. The Scriptures, and especially the
New Testament always associate this power through
which God acts creatively with the Spirit of God.
This Spirit is in the whole life of Christ. The Acts
summarize Jesus' activity with these words of Peter:
"You know the word which was proclaimed throughout all Judea, beginning from Galilee . . . how God
anointed Jesus of Nazareth with the Holy Spirit
and with power; how he went about doing good
and healing all that were oppressed by the devil, for
God was with him" (Acts 10:37; cf. Lk. 4:18-19). The
power of the Holy Spirit is thus intended when it
deals with the power of healing which emanates
from Christ (Lk. 5:17; 6:19; 8:46). The gift of healing
and the performing of miracles is mentioned by Paul
in the center of his list of diverse manifestations of
the Spirit (1 Cor. 12:7-11).

It is the same power of the Spirit which gives
strength to his word and confounds his audience.
"They were astonished at his teaching, for he taught

them as one who had authority, and not as the
scribes" (Mk. 1:21-22). It manifests itself especially
in the driving out of demons. Mark, who transmitted
the words of Matthew and Luke, sees these many
castings out of devils from the same point of view,
namely, that Jesus' mission is connected with the
dawn of the Kingdom (1:23-27; 3:11; 5:1, 20; 7:24-30;
9:14-19).

Because of the stress on the casting out of devils,
it would not be correct to consider them as purely
psychological cures. On the contrary, one might
claim that the Biblical interpretation rests on a lack
of medical knowledge. Since there was little knowledge about nature of mental diseases at that time,
it is said, the Bible attributes these diseases to the
power of the devil.

It would be derogatory to the meaning of Scripture
to consider mention of devils the result of insufficient
knowledge. When Christ addresses the evil spirit in
a diseased man, he uses a different approach than
would a doctor or psychiatrist. He points out what
is hidden beneath that which can be naturally ascer-
tained. He recognizes in the bodily vexation the
power of the evil one — satan, which cannot be
verified by science. The devil does not manifest
himself as a new reality on the borderline of natural
possibilities. He works through the natural, and
adapts himself to it. Christ, however, sees him as
the one who takes the word of God from the hearts
of men (Mk. 4:15), sows weeds in the field (Mt. 13:39)
and tyrannizes defenseless victims. In this light,

the healing of one possessed is not merely seen as a benefit to man — although it is this in high degree; it is rather an essential part of Jesus' engagement against the powers opposing the Kingdom of God. It is at the same time a visible sign of his victory. When his disciples returned from their mission and declared their joy that they had subdued devils in his name, Jesus identified with their joy and deepened it. It is good to rejoice for "I saw satan fall from heaven like lightning." The main idea is that this casting out of devils makes public the knowledge that satan, prince of devils and usurper of this world, is now stripped of his power. Although he is still bent on the ruin of man, his own destruction is, nevertheless, sealed. Jesus' word does not point to the event which took place before all time — satan's apostasy from God; it points to his destruction now, in time. The driving out of the devil is but a different symbol of what takes place on a high level hidden from us.

It belongs to the basic tenets of Jesus' mission-consciousness, that he might fight against satanic power. He did not come solely to teach a sublime truth, to point out the road to God, or to reform the religious attitudes of man. These would be ineffective if he did not radically conquer the powers which pursue a program bent on evil, which attempt to construct an anti-world against the new creation formed according to God's plan. For this reason he counteracts him as an irreconcilable and inexorable adversary who will not move. Whoever does

not concede this is so blinded by evil that he is pre-
pared to deny everything concerning Christ. He attributes to the unclean spirit what actually is the work
of the Holy Spirit. He sins therefore, not against
the Son of Man, but against the Holy Spirit himself
(Mt. 12:30-31).

The unclean spirits leave no doubt about the
situation in which they find themselves through
Christ's action: "What have you to do with us, Jesus
of Nazareth; have you come to destroy us? I know
who you are, the Holy One of God" (Mk. 1:24). This
forces spectators also to a question of conscience:
"What is this? A new teaching! With authority he
commands even the unclean spirits and they obey
him!" (Mk. 1:27-28). Here too an essential sequence
is obvious: eschatological action of the Lord leads to
the Christological question.

c. Miracles as responses to the Christological question

John the Baptist asks this Christological question
of Christ in the gospel in a positive and direct way.
Christ gives an unmistakable reply. He makes it
clear to all who listen that he claims he is the
Messiah, sent by God, with an exclusively religious
mission. This mission receives concrete form and
shape through the kerygma and salvific actions; the
nucleus, which is exactly the point in question, is
the redemptive nearness of God's dominion announcing itself actually and dynamically in his person.
Here is the text:

"Now when John heard in prison about the deeds

of the Christ, he sent word by his disciples and said
to him: Are you he who is to come, or shall we
look for another?" (Mt. 11:2-3; Lk. 18-20). "In that
hour he cured many of diseases and plagues and evil
spirits, and on many that were blind he bestowed
sight" (Lk. 7:21). "And Jesus answered them: Go and
tell John what you hear and see, the blind receive
their sight and the lame walk, lepers are cleansed
and the deaf hear, the dead are raised up and the
poor have good news preached to them. And blessed
is he who takes no offense at me" (Mt. 11:4-6; Lk.
7:22-23).

Are you he who is to come? John here reflects on
his own mission. He has introduced someone who
is stronger and greater than himself. He announced
only the final end; he who is to come would realize
the end itself. He threatened only with the judgment; he who is to come would actualize it.

John is completely in line with the prophets although he is a forerunner. His baptism is not yet a
salvific mediation. It is a sign of belonging to the
people who shall be saved through the penance they
perform; but it is not yet the eschatological salvation event itself. While the people see in Jesus only a
prophet, John accepts him as the Messiah, as he who
in reality is the salvific mediation of God. "Are you
he who is to come or shall we look for another?"
Why does John ask this? For the sake of his disciples?
Perhaps, but not only for that reason. Because he
himself has doubts about Christ? In either case
it is a question which concerns him personally.

Doubt might be too strong a word. John's question is more a nescience of what to think of a person, rather than a doubt. He cannot as yet grasp Jesus' course of action. The Messiah is to be the Powerful One who will baptize with the Holy Spirit and with fire. He has the flail in his hand and shall clean the threshing floor, gather the wheat and burn the chaff (cf. Mt. 3:11-12). For John there is first cleansing, judgment, destruction of the godless and, after that, salvation. Judgment and salvation are both preached; but judgment has the character of actuality, salvation lies in the future. John's question springs from a desire for the completion of his task: the glory of the Reign of God and indestructible righteousness on earth.

John does not see in Christ the baptism of fire, the punishing judgment. He misses in him success with the people and a clear confession of the Messiah. He sees nothing but patience, mercy and the endurance of injustice. How combine this with the Messiah symbol that the Baptist imagined?

Jesus gives an answer to this question, not directly and openly with "I am the Messiah," but by means of an appeal to the fulfillment of the prophecy. Meanwhile, he points out to the Baptist the characteristics of Messianic activity which his preaching lacks. The text which Jesus quotes is a combination of a number of texts from the Book of Isaiah, which has an eschatological and Messianic stance. This concentration of identical texts gives an extraordinary lucidity to Jesus' reply. He is the Messiah, for in him and through him is fulfilled what is written: "In that day, the deaf shall hear the words of a book, and out of their gloom and darkness the eyes of the blind shall see. The meek shall obtain fresh joy in the Lord, and the poor among men shall exult in the Holy One of Israel" (Is. 29:18-19).

"Behold your God will come with vengeance, with the recompense of God he will come and save you. Then the eyes of the blind shall be opened and the ears of the deaf unstopped; then shall the lame man leap like a hart, and the tongue of the dumb sing for joy" (Is. 35:4-6).

"The Lord has anointed me to bring good tidings to the afflicted; he has sent me to bind up the broken-hearted, to proclaim liberty to the captives, and the opening of the prison to those who are bound; to proclaim the year of the Lord's favor, and the Day of Vengeance of our God" (Is. 61:1-2).

Against the background of these texts what new meaning and content has Christ's answer? He is indeed the One to come, but in a way other than John imagined. The wrath of God which sounds through the prophecies (cf. Is. 35:4 and 61:2) does not pass his lips; he speaks only the announcement of salvation. The present is the time for the offering of grace; only in the future will come final salvation or condemnation. For him the dominion of God is, first of all, the realization of his redemptive will, of his assisting love for what is lost and defective. In short, the Kingdom fashions — and is — redemption;

it is the recapitulation and envelopment of all salvation. There are therefore phases in which the Kingdom realizes itself. It is not yet a settled order that dominates; it is something that has a beginning in the world, develops, grows and increases. "Kingdom of God" means God rules and brings his influence to bear. Since other powers dominate men, the Kingdom of God can only be established through redemption. Because man was fatally wounded in soul and body through sin, the Kingdom of God can only come through forgiveness of sin. Because through sin he was condemned to destruction, to death and associated bodily and spiritual disintegration, disease and suffering, the Kingdom of God can therefore come only through abolition of these, and by transformation into immortality. The Kingdom shall come when man's alienation has given way to new integration in God. Where the divine power breaks through, there forgiveness, healing, sanctification, new creation take place.

By presenting his miracles as the fulfillment of the Messianic-eschatological prophecies Christ makes John realize that the healing, casting out of demons and raising from the dead belong to the breakthrough of the Kingdom of God. This does not mean that the prophecies to which he appeals find their total fulfillment in physical miracles; it does mean that these too belong to the fulfillment, as anticipating symbols, as pointing to a more embracing reality. It is true that Jesus takes a strong stand against the Judaic conviction that all disease springs from the sin of the sufferer or his parents (cf. the question of the disciples concerning the man born blind in Jn. 9:2); this does not deny that this misconception is ultimately based on the truth that disease and sin are essentially related. In all the Biblical testimonies, disease is interference in the order of creation, a result of the Fall and a remembrance of it. But it is clear that when the curse is taken away through the new creation of heaven and earth liberation from disease results. The entire man belongs to God. Therefore man is redeemed as a unity of body and soul, in his entire humanity. The lame man not only hears the words "Your sins are forgiven" but also "Rise up, take up your bed and go home." The power and mercy of God are not restricted to reversal and cleansing of the spirit; they affect the body too. A miracle thus becomes a visible expression of total restoration, a sign that sin is being weakened.

The combat with sin reaches its zenith in Jesus' engagement with death. Through victory over death he recreates human life. Our death results from the way we possess life. Dying accentuates what our life has really been all the time. By conquering death the dimension of our life changes, life achieves the state of imperishability; once again it is communicating with God. In Christ's eyes miracles are signs of the Kingdom, not merely as announcements of the coming reign, but as expressions of a reign already present. They are signs of redemption in the full sense of the word, but with reference to a total fulfillment yet to come. A healing miracle which reaches its climax in the raising from the dead, is

itself redemption. That blind see, deaf hear, lame
walk and dead rise, is the dawn of the new creation,
which becomes reality with our resurrection and
glorification. It is a beginning which raises expectations of completion; it is a pledge as well which in
some degree brings the expected to realization. A
miracle belongs to the order of salvation and for
that reason its existence is something normal. Nevertheless, all regularity is lacking in its presentation.
To this extent it is extraordinary and incomprehen-
sible. By way of miracles the Kingdom breaks
through only here and there like lightning; this makes
the horizon of God's plan of salvation momentarily
visible and later leaves it in the dark again.

4.   Miracles — divine invitations to believe in Jesus Christ

The gospel miracle is an eschatological sign; it is
also a sign that gives testimony to the Person of
Jesus.[12]

In the eschatological perspective the Person of
Jesus is the center. His preaching of the Kingdom
of God and his deeds of salvation are interconnected
and complement each other in a unity filled with
meaning. His word effects redemption in the miracle. His Miracles are indeed the Kingdom of God.
Jesus not only preaches the Kingdom; he makes it
present in his deeds. Its actuality is not to be merely
proclaimed in and through Jesus' action. God has
bound its realization to the mission of Christ. God
uses him for the last and definitive offer of salvation:
"Be converted and believe the glad tidings." With

this, man is inevitably placed before a decision which will be salutary or fatal for him. Because God has bound his salvation to the Christ, we see why the answer to John ends with the warning words: "Blessed is he who takes no offense at me" (Mt. 11:6). In contrast to the allocutions of a prophet, the belief which Jesus demands goes further than just his word. Jesus reveals himself in preaching the very content of the salvific message. Hence, not just his words, but especially his Person becomes a challenge: Christ presents himself as the salvation expected from God; man wants salvation, but he resists the concrete form in which it becomes reality. He had imagined it to be something entirely different; now that he is face-to-face with it, he raises objections. This humanizing of the divine cannot be proper! How can a man arrogate such a thing to himself? No, God cannot demand that I believe this! Here begins the parting of the ways. Should one sacrifice his opinion? This is possible only for a person in love and faith. Or shall his lack of understanding manifest itself in disbelief and rancor?

In Nazareth this opposition finds striking expression. There Jesus also appeals to the fact that the Scriptures find fulfillment in him. But precisely his own city considers it intolerable to accept his presence. He who is so like every one else, whose family is known so well — how can he be God's elected? This is the sting of unreasonable resistance which comes from satan. Christ calls him blessed who gives his credence. For this reason appeals to his preaching and to his miracles. The latter are

part of his testimony. It is a divine guarantee which
marks the human witness, a testimony from God
which must be seen as being indissolubly one with
the witness of the word and lends it an increased
persuasiveness: "The Lord worked with them and
attested the word through the miracles which accompanied them" (Mk. 16:20). A miracle is the exterior
demonstration of divine revelation.

Why has this miracle witness such high value?
Actually, because of human weakness which is not
able to estimate the moral value of another person
from a proper inner conviction and desire for the good
— not even when, as in Christ, this takes on the character of a moral miracle. Hence physical miracles, as
testimony of his word, help to bridge the gap
between Christ and his audience. In this sense
Christ appeals to the miracle signs.

Per se, faith through miracle is a detour. To believe only on the strength of signs betrays a lack of
confidence. Faith finds its basis in the person in
whom one believes. Even though man by himself
can learn a great deal about his fellow man, there
is in every one an inscrutable core which can be laid
bare only through free communication; the other
can believe or not believe this. Faith is justified only
on the strength of trustworthiness. Its foundation is
the testifying person himself — his character, his
honesty, his unselfishness, his loyalty and love. To
believe someone's word is in fact to accept the person
himself. This is possible, insofar as this person is
the reasonable justification for this committment.

Bornkamm's qualities were miracles ?? No

It is moreover necessary that he evidence his trustworthiness for the duration of the commitment. This must express itself in signs capable of confirming the opinion of the other. This is especially needed regarding the most hazardous form of belief: belief in the love of someone else.

John the Baptist bore witness and demanded belief in his message, without performing any sign. Christ too bore witness. His message includes miracles which are an essential part of it. This makes it possible to allow miracles to fulfill a function in regard to his person. But the purest belief is that in which he himself is deemed sufficient for man, as John pictures the first disciples who came to Jesus (Jn. 1:35-52). Miracle as confirmation and sanction of Christ's person and mission finds striking expression in the healing of the paralytic (Mk. 2:1-12 and par.). Forgiving of sins cannot be seen, only believed. Healing of the body, however, can be seen, and indeed as an act of God who makes the word of healing credible: "But that you may know that the Son of Man has authority on earth to forgive sins — he said to the paralytic — I say to you, rise, take up your pallet and go home." The presence which Christ asserts can be believed from the miracle as credible. Hence the reproach for the cities which perished in their unbelief: "Then he began to upbraid the cities, where most of his mighty works had been done, because they did not repent. Woe to you Chorazin! Woe to you Bethsaida! For if the mighty works done in you had been done in Tyre and Sidon they would have repented long ago in sackcloth and ashes. But I tell you it shall be more tolerable on the Day of Judgment for Tyre and Sidon, than for you" (Mt. 11:20-22).

Christ performs signs to arouse faith; but he refuses signs demanded on grounds of unbelief. The pharisees are not satisfied with Jesus' miracles; they make demands: they desire a simple sign straight from heaven, which would force them to recognition of the truth. These miracles do not convince them. Jesus refuses because the miracles he has performed are testimonials of his mission.

The Synoptic versions are not the same, but they agree in broad outline. Mark is apodictic. "Truly, I say to you, no sign shall be given to this generation" (Mk. 8:12). Matthew and Luke read: "But no sign shall be given to it except the sign of the Prophet Jonah" (Mt. 12:39; 16:2; Lk. 11:29). Both however, interpret differently. Luke identifies the salvific preaching of Jonah with Christ. The whole of Jesus' activity for his people is the sign that is given them. In Matthew the story of Jonah in the belly of the whale serves as a "type" for Christ's resurrection. This is the only sign that is given them. Both interpretations mean that the sign demanded by the Jews is refused. The reason is their unbelief and their disloyalty to God. Very properly Christ calls them, in accord with Old Testament phraseology, an adulterous generation.

Christ clearly teaches that the sign which he has given is sufficient for those who are willing to believe. For one who lacks this readiness and obstinately

of freedom

resists, a miracle is of no value. He receives, however, no forcing sign; a miracle is not a spell which places man under compulsion. It does not thrust faith on man. This would be absolutely contradictory to the interpersonal relationship to which revelation aims. Faith on God's side is a claim to which every one must respond individually, since he is personally addressed. The sign directs itself to understanding; but it especially appeals to the will which accepts it with free accord as a sign from God. The insight that it is God who gives the sign does not follow from strictly rational proofs; it is experienced quasi-intuitively and interpreted from a certain inner aspiration to God. This truly means that it is a gift from God: "No one comes to me, unless the Father draws him." It is sin to shut oneself out because in so doing one extinguishes the light of truth. For this reason Jesus left his antagonists and departed (Mk. 8:13).

The same situation obtains in Nazareth. "And he did not do many mighty works there, because of their unbelief" (Mt. 13:58; Mk. 6:5-6). Luke states it on a broader scale: "He said to them, Doubtless you will quote to me this proverb — Physician heal yourself — what we have heard you did at Capharnaum do here also in your own country" (Lk. 4:23-24).

This means that Jesus must perform some miracles in Nazareth, as he did elsewhere, and so prove to the sceptical minded that he is the Messiah. Here too he rejects the demand for miracles. Belief that asks for miracles is no true belief, because the attitude with which they meet his person is not one of

true humility but of intolerance. Thus the miracle
has become, in principle, impossible.

Consequently it is entirely consistent that Jesus
praises a believing attitude toward himself, and that
he demands belief before he performs a miracle (Mk.
2:5; 5:34, 36; 9:23; 10:52). With this the apparent
contradiction, which would oppose two facts, disap-
pears; the miracle will elicit faith, and belief is demanded preceding the miracle.

Faith as presupposition for miracle means that one
believes Jesus on his own recognizance. It is the
condition required for precise interpersonal rela-
tions — compassion, openness, frankness. A miracle
affirms this trust in his person and can grow into
real belief of salvation. This wavering medium between a desire to believe and a not-yet-complete
decision of faith, is what prompted the father of
the possessed to exclaim: "I believe Lord, help Thou
my unbelief" (Mk. 9:24). Where frankness is missing,
demand for a miracle is a sign of unbelief; it may
originate from a friendly or coldly neutral attitude.
Belief forced on man through signs is absolutely
without value from a religious point of view, and
is dismissed by Jesus as are all show-miracles. Thus
the miracle is immediately connected with Jesus'
claim, his person and mission. In the last instance
the issue is his person. This demands decision.
The miracle is only part of the common scandal to
which his person is exposed. Not the miracle but he,
himself, is the sign of contradiction, the stone to be
tripped over or upon which to build (Lk. 2:34).

3

MIRACLES AS PREACHING
AND TEACHING IN THE GOSPEL
ACCORDING TO MATTHEW

The New Testament is the message of Jesus, given
to us by his disciples. This has not literally come to
us in its present historically accepted form. We
note the unique situation that the disciples did not,
or at least not completely, understand him or his
teaching during his public life. It was only when
he encountered them in a new manner of existence,
as a power reality filled with the Spirit of God, that
they learned from the resurrection to accept on
faith, all that happened before. The word that
reaches us first took form in their belief.

More important than this, their preaching took
place in an altered situation.[13] It concerned those who
had heard the call from Christ and answered it. It
was passed on within a believing community. This
community was in need of a deepening of the Christ
image; it was a probing of their own structure and
culture, a desire to defend and explain their belief
before bystanders; it was seeking solutions to a
number of problems. The image of the word as it
reaches us is therefore formulated in accord with

the concrete situation in which it was then enunciated
and recorded. That this nevertheless remains the
authentic word of Christ is possible only because
Christ is not just the Christ "yesterday" but also the
Christ "today." What he said yesterday, he says
now too. This message "now" is identical with the
preaching "then," because it is the same Christ who
through his Spirit speaks in the Church.

When Matthew speaks to the Judaic-Christian
communities which came into existence in Palestine
after the ascension of the Lord, he directs his message of the Gospel to them in the word that received
its stature from the Christ "now." He talks about
authority which the Lord has given his Church; he
gives response to the question as to who Christ is,
and who will be part of the Kingdom of God; he
stresses belief in the Lord as the only way to salvation and also opens this way to the gentiles.

Matthew illustrates this from the life of Jesus.
Jesus and the twelve with whom he is present, in
whose company he acts, who defends them against
malicious questioners — this is the same situation as
his Church experiences now. He is with them, acts
in power in their favor. From him, too, comes the
answer to those who oppose them. In short, he is
the Lord and Helper of his Church now as he was
then with his disciples. Although the other evangelists show a noticeable tension between the message
of Christ and the translation of this message for the
use of the faithful — this is especially clear in the
parables — Matthew consistently shows a tendency

to make the preaching an instruction. This is also found in a number of the miracle stories. Their eschatological message must allow for instruction based on them.

What perspectives are now opened by this didactic tendency in the preaching of the miracles?[14]

1. The systematic construction of the gospel of Matthew

In the first part of his gospel Matthew replaces Mark's not too accurate chronology with a systematic classification of the data. Beginning with the prophetic call of Christ he composes a moral program and makes it grow into one great instruction (Sermon on the Mount: Chapters 5-7). The same can be said of the parables which formed the main element of Jesus' preaching to the people. In systematic order the miracles are compiled in two chapters (8 and 9); they overpower the reader with their impressive number. Nevertheless, this system, which is only a technical formulation, would not interest us further if the materials produced in the separate chapters were not mutually involved. On closer view, the Sermon on the Mount and the miracle narratives seem to form one whole. This is clearly shown by the framework of the verses (Mt. 4:23 and 9:35) which give a general view of Jesus' activity. We read: "And he went about all Galilee (about all the cities and villages (9:35) teaching in their synagogues and preaching the gospel of the Kingdom, healing every disease and every infirmity among the people."

This general information about Jesus' "works" in word and deed immediately before the Sermon on the Mount and after his miracle stories, indicates that the evangelist, at the beginning of his gospel, not only introduces the Christ to us as the Messiah of the "Word," but also as the Messiah of the "Deed" who underlines and confirms his salvific doctrine through his salvation activity. Matthew's miracle narratives thus strengthen his concept of, and witness to, the Christ; in other words, the miracle narratives have a Christological meaning and significance. This becomes even more evident from analysis of chapters 8 and 9 and their relationship with the general context. A first cycle is formed by Matthew 8:2-17. Here mention is made of healings explained from reference to Is. 53:4: "He has borne our griefs and carried our sorrows."

A second cycle emerges from 9:18-31. The theme here is faith as expressed in verse 22, "Your faith has made you whole," and verse 29, "According to your faith be it done to you."

Verses 9:32-34 are meant to close the cycle. This is not merely a matter of healing a deaf and dumb man possessed by the devil; more important is the reaction which Christ's action provokes. The crowd's response is surprise: "Never was anything like this seen in Israel." The pharisees express their rejection: "He casts out demons by the prince of demons." The miracles force the viewers to take a stand in regard to the Christological problem.

Further grouping is not so clearly noticeable. This is possibly explained by the fact that Matthew borrowed his material from the Mark tradition, and thus included selections, which Mark placed before or after a miracle story.

The intermediate text, Matthew 8:18 — 9:17, contains some miracle narratives which throw light on new aspects: Christ's power over demons, his authority to forgive sins; but another theme is also introduced which might be entitled "Lord and Discipleship." The disposition and attitude of Jesus' disciples is continuously shown from 4:23 to 9:35. Chapter 10 presents them as cooperators and their activity includes, besides the preaching of the Kingdom (10:7), the performing of all the miracles mentioned in chapters 8 and 9: "And he called to him, his twelve disciples and gave them authority over unclean spirits, to cast them out and to heal every disease and every infirmity" (10:1); and further, "Heal the sick, raise the dead, cleanse the lepers, cast out demons" (10:8).

There is a close affinity between Matthew 10 and Matthew 5 and 9. The twelve take part in Jesus' Messianic mission and authority. The connection with 5 and 9 continues in chapter 10 to 11:2-6. Since in some chapters Matthew introduced Jesus as the Christ, the decisive question is — and it is the question asked by the Baptist: "Are you he who is to come, or shall we look for another?" (Mt. 11:3; cf. 12:23). The subsequent course of the gospel shows that this is the decisive question. Jesus introduces his own person and mission by referring to the Baptist (Mt. 11:7-19). He thunders his "woes" against the impenitent cities of Galilee for not listening to his preaching and for refusing to see his works (11:20-24). He lets no occasion pass to point out to the scribes and pharisees their unbelief, and to convince them of his mission and authority (12:1-45).

On the other hand, he calls his disciples blessed, because the Father has shown them his revelation (11:25). Because of their real faith he calls them his relatives (12:48-50). When division of minds is brought about in the hearing and understanding of the parables, he explains to his disciples: "To you it has been given to know the secrets of the Kingdom of Heaven, but to them it has not been given" (13:11).

The question of the Baptist thus performs a very important function. It is, through Christ's answer, a finalization of the Christological theme developed in the preceding chapters and carried on in those that follow. One might possibly ask why the request of the Baptist and the answer of Christ are not immediately connected with Matthew 9:35. Chapter 10 seems to break the natural sequence. But this is only in appearance. That the "blind see and the lame walk, lepers are cleansed and the dead are raised up and the poor have the good news preached to them" (Mt. 11:5), is also the work of his disciples by virtue of their mission through him. This belongs therefore, essentially to the understanding of the Christological theme of the Matthew Gospel: Jesus is not only the God-sent Christ in word and

deed; he is also the Lord of his Church, who makes
his disciples share in his full powers. In other words,
he is the one sent by God and at the same time the
one who sends. "As the Father has sent me so I
send you" (Jn. 17:26). He identifies himself with his
disciples in such way that who receives them, receives him (Mt. 10:40).

SUMMARY: Within the framework of Matthew 4:17,
where Jesus begins his activity, and Matthew 11:6,
where he answers the decisive question of the Baptist, the miracle narratives contribute to understanding Christ. They show Jesus:

a). As the fulfillment of the Old Testament prophecies and as the servant of God acting with
power and filled with compassion.

b). As the lord and helper of his disciples and
community, who makes them share in his own
fullness of power.

2. The thematic of the miracles

a. Miracles as the Christological fulfillment of Scripture

Besides the reply of Jesus to John (Mt. 11:4-6)
Matthew has placed the pericope 8:2-17 in the light
of the Old Testament portent, this time as the fulfillment of the word of Isaiah 53:4. "He has borne our
griefs" etc. It refers to the suffering servant of
Yahweh, a figure which obtained its full stature in
Christ.

The Christological theme of 8:2-17, is recognized
not merely by the Scriptural quotation; it speaks

from the text of the pericope itself. The centurion
of Capernaum by his words draws an impressive
picture of the fullness of the power of Jesus which
is without equal in the other miracle narratives:
"Lord, I am not worthy to have you come under my
roof, but only say the word and my servant will be
healed. For I am a man under authority, with sol-
diers under me and I say to one, Go and he goes,
and to another Come and he comes, and to my
slave, Do this and he does it" (8:8-9). What is the
meaning of these words? Just as the centurion, himself only a subordinate, can order and dictate his
commands, so Jesus possesses a like but much greater
competence. He can make higher powers subject to
his will and word, so that he himself need not come
to the house of the centurion. This confession gives
proof of a faith in Jesus' person which he seeks in
vain in Israel. The healing is not of prime importance
for Matthew; it is the confession, which reveals
Christ to us, which is.

Matthew 8:16 considers the fullness of power mentioned in 8:8. "That evening they brought to him
many, who were possessed with demons, and he
cast out the spirits with a word, and healed all who
were sick!" The leper (8:1-4) speaks of the wonderful
power of Jesus, who needs only to will it in order
to perform the miracle: "Lord if you will, you can
make me clean" (8:3). The same is true for the healing of the centurion's servant. Matthew is more
interested in the fullness of the power of Jesus'
person, than in his acting as a worker of miracles.

But to revert to the quotation — Matthew would have us understand that miracles themselves do not possess a conclusive force to convince us of the dignity and mission of Jesus. The proof that the Scriptures — and the will of God — are fulfilled, gives the real Christological meaning. Matthew wants to show that the miracles of Jesus are deeds performed out of obedience; therefore they must be understood as a legitimate part of his Messianic task and mission. To accomplish this he endowed the systematic structure of chapters 5-9 with an intrinsic parallel. Just as the Messiah "of the word" declares at the beginning of his preaching that he has come not to do away with the law and the prophets but to fulfill them (Mt. 5:17), so the Messiah "of the work" at the beginning of his miracle-works shows that it is he who fulfills the Scriptures. This is not chance parallel; it is motivated by the composition of 5-9 itself. Preaching and miracles are unfolded as two facets of his works. Both therefore serve explicitly as justification for the fulfillment of the Scriptures. The story of the healing of the leper receives a still newer meaning from its background. We read there: "Go show thyself to the priest and offer the gift that Moses demanded, for a sign to the people" (8:4). One could understand that the purpose of this command is that priest and people would be made certain about the healing, and in one accord be brought to acknowledgement of him who brings it about with one authoritative word. But it is more plausible that obedience to the law be emphasized. Thus the command of Jesus affirms the testimony he gave of himself in his Sermon on the Mount (5:17).

How does Matthew 8:17, understand Isaiah 53:4:
"He has borne our grief and carried our sorrows?"
In the context of Isaiah, this verse means that in our
behalf the suffering servant of Yahweh takes upon
himself our sufferings, weaknesses and defections; he
does this as propitiation for our sins, which are the
ultimate cause of our miserable state. In 8:17, however, Matthew interprets the "taking upon himself"
of our misery, as a taking away, and the "bearing"
as a carrying away; actually, he has bodily healing
and casting out of demons in mind. In 8:17, there
is no question of any substitute suffering for a
diseased person: the text does not suggest that Jesus
himself became ill. On the contrary, he is the powerful Lord who frees others from their diseases. There
is a relationship with the initial meaning of this word;
redemption, through his reconciling suffering and
death, now has as a consequence release from the
burden of infirmities and the fetters of satan. Both
works testify that in Christ the Kingdom of God has
come, and that his powers are active in this world.
The service of his mission (cf. Is. 53) is also seen to
full advantage in Matthew 8:17: the power Christ
possesses is totally at the service of his being called
to the expelled, despised and infirm man. This is
illustrated by the healing of a leper, a gentile and
a sick woman. The purpose of this message is that
the community learns to see how he reveals himself
with power as the merciful Lord. Hence Matthew
completes, elsewhere, the invocation **Kyrie** (Lord) or
Son of David with an **Eleison**, "have mercy on us."

This last notion is confirmed by another Scriptural

quotation from Hosea 6:6: "For I desire steadfast love and not sacrifice." This text is part of a statement of Jesus about his mission: "For I come not to call the righteous but sinners" (9:13). This explanation about his mission is a response to the question of the pharisees, "Why does your teacher eat with tax collectors and sinners?" (9:11); it is also a justification of his action in the calling of Levi — Matthew. By relating this Hosea quotation to himself, Jesus wants his antagonists to understand that by doing so he fulfills the will of God as enunciated in Hosea. Jesus' main reason, according to Matthew, is not so much to point out the commandment of mercy to the pharisees; he wishes to assure them that he fulfills the Scriptures, and thus proves that he is the Christ. His mercy too proves his Messianic mission. Therefore Matthew frequently mentions this mercy (9:36; 14:14; 15:32; 20:34).

b. The Lord and Helper in his Church

The miracles mentioned by Matthew have a Christological meaning. They also have an ecclesiological theme. In line with the latter, Matthew presents the life of Jesus Christ as that of one who solves problems with authority. In 9:2-17 he places the three together. Matthew 9:2-8 is a matter of dispute with the scribes over the authority for forgiveness of sins, called forth through the healing of a paralytic. The point of contention is solved by an act of Jesus' power. Matthew (as is evident from the parallel with Mark/Luke) reduced this miracle story to a minimum. Fullness of authority is of prime importance: "But

that you may know, that the Son of Man has authority on earth to forgive sins — he then said to the
paralytic, Rise up, take your bed and go home" (9:6).
This is also apparent in the conclusion, proper to
Matthew: "When the crowds saw that, they were
afraid and they glorified God, who had given such
authority to men" (9:8). The praise indeed concerns
the miracle, but even more the authority shown
therein.

The conclusion is especially striking: ". . . who had
given such authority to men." The plural form indicates that the Church draws her power to forgive
sins from Jesus. The Christological there has assumed
an ecclesiastical aspect. Jesus' words, "As the Father
has sent me, so I send you" here assume a concrete
form. Christ thus is the one sent with authority; he
also grants authority.

Another important point is mentioned in the pericope concerning the centurion from Capernaum
(8:5-13) and the Canaanite woman (15:21-28). Both
cases deal with the healing of non-Jews, performed
at a distance. Faith plays a unique part in the
achieved healing.

15:21-28: "And Jesus went away from there and
withdrew to the district of Tyre and Sidon. And
behold a Canaanite woman from the region came
out and cried, Have mercy on me O Lord, Son of
David, my daughter is severely possessed by a demon.
But he did not answer her a word. And his disciples
came and begged him saying: Send her away, for

she is crying after us. He answered, I was sent only
to the lost sheep of Israel. But she came and knelt
before him saying, Lord help me and he answered,
It is not fair to take the children's bread and throw
it to the dogs. She said: Yes Lord, yet even the dogs
eat the crumbs that fall from their master's table.
Then Jesus answered her: O woman great is your
faith; Be it done to you as you desire. And her
daughter was healed instantly."

The sincerity of this word cannot be doubted.
Such particularism would not have found favor at
a time when the Church was beginning her work
among the gentiles. In Mark, however, we find a
weakened version: "Let the children **first** be fed"
(Mk. 7:27). Matthew stresses the precedence of
Israel. This could indicate that Christ's mission would
seem restricted to Israel. Nevertheless, the story
takes a different turn than was presumed in the
beginning. Jesus helps, regardless. This means that
healing as an eschatological gift and, as sign and
commencement of the time of salvation, is not limited
to Israel; it can also fall to the lot of the gentiles.
The one condition is faith. In spite of the strong
particularistic character of his word, the evangelist
makes it clear that the mission to the gentiles, as a
legitimate development in the Church, can be traced
to Christ himself. Mark therefore stresses that his
gentile Christians, for whom he writes, must acknowl-
edge the precedence of the Jewish nation (cf. Rom.
11). Matthew however, softens the strict Jewish
standpoint, but makes it clear to his Christians that

faith opens the way to Christ — for the gentiles too.
The story of the centurion at Capernaum offers us,
in broad outline, the same conclusion. Here too,
Christ is won over by the faith of the gentiles.
Matthew relates this healing to the word which Luke
mentions elsewhere, but which renders the meaning
and his interpretation of this narrative: "I tell you
that many will come from the east and the west and
sit at table with Abraham, Isaac and Jacob in the
Kingdom of Heaven; while the sons of the Kingdom
will be thrown into outer darkness, then men will
weep and gnash their teeth" (Mt. 8:11-13).

Matthew interprets the faith of the centurion as
a promise of Jesus to the gentiles and at the same
time as a word of judgment over Israel. From the
words and works of Christ himself, he wants to prove
the validity of the admission of the gentiles into the
Church.

Jesus is not just the Christ who answers the
question of authority posed to himself and to his
disciples; he is not just the authentic starting point
of a number of developments which operate in the
Church; but he is also the omnipotent Lord who is
open to the suppliant prayer of his disciples. This is
the third instruction, which Matthew has in view
in the miracle report. By presenting the miracle to
his readers as an answer to prayer, the evangelist
gives them the certainty that faithful supplication to
the glorified Lord offers possibility of contact with
him who provides help. This thought is further
developed in Matthew 8:23-27 and in the pericope
dealing with a similar situation, Mt. 14:22-33.

We read there: "And when he got into the boat, his disciples followed him. And behold there arose a great storm on the sea, so that the boat was being swamped by the waves; but he was asleep. And they went and woke him saying, Save us, Lord, we are perishing. And he said to them: Why are you afraid, O men of little faith? Then he arose and rebuked the winds and the sea, and there was a great calm. And the men marvelled saying: What sort of man is this, that even the wind and sea obey him?" (8:23-27).

In his narrative Mark accuses the disciples of unbelief. "Why are you afraid? Have you yet no faith?" There is a harsh reproach in these words. The little word "yet" especially makes one feel that the disciples disappoint him. The meaning of the reprimand is this: Has company with me and seeing the great works of God not opened your eyes? Do you still not know who I am?

In Matthew, the reply of Jesus is much softer. First of all the reproachful word "yet" is omitted; furthermore, unbelief is changed into pusillaimity.

Another distinction strikes us: in contrast with Mark, Matthew formulates the cry for help as an ejaculatory prayer, "Lord save us, we perish!" Mark expressed the pressing need for help in a question: "Teacher, do you not care if we perish?" Instead of "Teacher" Matthew uses "Lord" — the title given to Christ by the early community because of his resurrection and divine glory. **Kyrie**, Lord, is therefore

the majestic title with which the Christian utters his
faith in the Glorified One; it is this confession which
characterizes him as a disciple.

This distinction between the two authors shows
up more clearly in the pericope of Matthew 14:22-33
(Mk. 6:45-52) which tells of Jesus walking upon the
water. Mark points to the attitude of the disciples
as a sign of unwisdom: "And he got into the boat
with them and the wind ceased. And they were
utterly astounded, for they did not understand about
the loaves, but their hearts were hardened." Matthew
however explicitly connects a confession of faith
of the disciples with this episode: "And when they
(Jesus and Peter) got into the boat, the wind ceased.
And those in the boat worshiped him saying: Truly
you are the Son of God."

Matthew again stresses the power of faithful supplication made by Jesus' disciples. The pericope
shows the magnitude of the promise given to the
faith of the disciples in following Christ. Matthew
does not suppress the inability of the disciples to
hold fast to this faith through their own power in
face of difficulties. But with the demand to follow
him, the Lord also offers his disciples indispensable
help.

How can we explain why Mark and Matthew,
relating the same event, develop such contrary opin-
ions? According to Mark the disciples are and
remain lacking in understanding; in Matthew an
affirmation of faith follows. Which of the two evan-

gelists is correct? The solution is not difficult, as long as we take the disposition and purpose proper to the evangelist into account. From the fulfillment of Christ's life in his resurrection and his glory the disciples came to understand who he really was and the things that happened in his life. The whole of the New Testament is written in this newly acquired light, from an understanding brought to clarity through the Spirit of Christ. The purpose which Mark pursues in his gospel, however, is to show that Jesus' true nature could be understood only after the resurrection, and that this belief in him as the Son of God, presupposes belief in his resurrection.

Mark places Jesus' appearance against the background of the concepts which they have about his person. People, pharisees and disciples pass in review, and faith is lacking in all. The people are too superficial, the pharisees are to obdurate in their theology and conception of the Law. And the disciples? They do believe in him as the one sent from God, they put their trust in him — but this, for Mark, is not yet real faith. They hope for a realization of their trusted expectation and do not see that totally different reality which God decrees to establish in and through Christ. Hence in the eyes of Mark, the disciples, all during the earthly life of the Lord and even immediately after his resurrection, are disciples who do not believe, who do not understand, who do not see. He applies this resolutely to all situations.

Matthew has a different approach. For him as

well, worthwhile belief in Jesus, is possible only
after acceptance of the resurrection. He sees the
disicples, however, as the figure of the Church. They
are the first believers. Their faith is now projected
back into their association with Christ during his
earthly life. From the fulfillment, already during
his earthly life, they are the Church and therefore,
believers. This is expressed very clearly in specific
cases. The confession of Peter in Caesarea Philippi
without doubt forms the culminating point. The
evangelist, however, uses Jesus' appearance in the
middle of the lake to allow for the disciples' demonstration of faith in their master. In the same situation where, according to Mark, Christ reproaches
his disciples for their lack of understanding and
obduracy of heart, Matthew stresses their confession
of belief in the Son of God and their prostration
which is the sign of adoration. Nevertheless there is
also a dissonance in Matthew's account: a sign that
he has not forgotten the original situation. As in
Matthew 8:26 so in Matthew 14:31, Christ rebukes
the disciples for their weak faith. We find this in
other places too (cf. Mt. 16:8; 17:20). This has a
purpose within the ecclesiological stance of the
author.

A disciple of Jesus is one who believes in him
and accepts his revelation. This is an essential part
of being a disciple. In that faith there is possibility
of growth, room for vacillation, lack of trust etc.
Faint hearted faith is not unbelief, not deviation
from Christ; nevertheless, it bespeaks a deficiency

within the state of being faithful, a failing in the following of Christ. Many in the Church have to wrestle with this: Matthew well knows that all that glitters is not gold. It is difficult to experience the Lord when absent or even when he is present. But he is always near his Church, near his disciples and he helps them with his intervention. Faith in the presence and power of the glorified Lord must strengthen the faith of the faint-hearted and fortify their weak trust. The purpose of many of Matthew's miracle stories is to confirm the community in faith in the Lord of the Church. This is the real reason why the description of the miracle itself is often reduced to a minimum (cf. Mt. 9:20-22; with Mk. 5:25-34; Mt. 9:23-26 with Mk. 5:35-43; Mt. 17:14-20 with Mk. 9:23-26). The narrative is reduced to a few stereotyped formulas: the supporting cast is shortened so that only two persons remain: Jesus and the one who asks, or for whom the miracle is performed. In the center stands the dialogue, with faith as conversation matter. Faith is usually expressed in a prayer. Man facing Christ is a prayerful and beseeching creature — not, as in Mark, a fear oppressed woman (Mk. 5:53) or a doubting and desperate father (Mk. 9:22). Although the other evangelist also mentions that Jesus performs miracles for those who believe, no one has made prayerful faith so strongly the central point of his account as Matthew. From Jesus' viewpoint, the healing is likewise underlined as an answer to prayer (Mt. 8:13; 9:22; 9:29; 15:28). Matthew moreover gives prayer the character of adoration through prostration and the addressing title **Kyrie.** This adoring and prayerful faith is **the** attitude of the community toward its Lord, whose commanding majesty can do all things (Mt. 8:2; 9:18; 14:33; 15:25; 20:20; 28:9-17).

The interpretation given by Matthew to the miracle narratives constitutes an important advance for Biblical preaching. Here again it is obvious that what Scripture has to tell us is not only preaching but also teaching. Jesus and his disciples put both into practice from the beginning. Matthew uses Jesus' word and his works; his miracles preferably are to be regarded from this dual viewpoint. This enabled him to deepen the faith of his Christians and to bring them, through a pastoral stimulus, to a more trustful practice of faith.

4

MIRACLES AS SIGNS AND SYMBOLS
IN JOHN'S GOSPEL

1. John's manner of consideration

John's gospel allows the reader to acquaint himself with seven miracles from the life of Christ: the miracle of the wine at Cana (2:1-11), the healing of the dying son of the centurion also at Cana (4:34-53), the healing of the lame man in Bethsaida (5:1-9), the multiplication of the bread (6:1-13), the walking on the lake (6:16-21), the healing of the man born blind (9:1-41), and the raising of Lazarus from the dead (11:1-44).[15] The multiplication of the bread and the walking on the lake are also a part of the synoptic tradition; the healing at Cana is, if not identical, at least a variant of the healing of the centurion's servant at Capernaum (Mt. 8:5-13); the healing of the man born blind, of the lame man and the raising of Lazarus from the dead have their parallel in other gospels. Only the miracle of the wine is missing, although there is an analogy in the miracle of the bread. John selected these seven miracles from the many which Jesus performed in the presence of his disciples (20:30).

The difference between John and the other gospels does not lie in the fact that he mentions miracles entirely different from the synoptic miracles in regard to their empirical aspect; the difference lies in the meaning. This again must not be misunderstood, as if he interprets in an essentially different way than they. On the contrary, he pursues the first catechetical line; but what does not clearly show through "there" is a theologically meaningful "here." In the synoptics, miracles have a Christological meaning too; they possess a prophetic aspect and arouse deep faith in Christ. But in John all this is brought out in sharper relief; the background against which he projects his images is on a consistently deeper plane than is found in the synoptics. Mark looks back from the resurrection to Christ's appearance, and characterizes him as the hidden Son of Man, who even now shall remain hidden from every unbeliever. Matthew sees him especially as the Lord and the powerful presence in his Church. For Luke he remains the charity and benevolence of God. For all three the coming of the Kingdom of God is the great event in which Jesus' appearance is concerned. Who he in fact is remains veiled, though not opaque. John makes it explicitly his task to give an insight into the person of Jesus. In doing so, the Kingdom of God as an event falls into the background. All events are used to reveal who he is, and what he means to us. John's point of view is governed by the figure of Christ entering into his glory. Jesus' life is a going out from the Father in order to return into heaven to his Father to be glorified by him. With

almost infinite repetition this theme returns and
returns.[16] What is John trying to say? To throw light
on Jesus' origin and being, he points not to the
Incarnation but rather to the glorification. His entrance into glory makes manifest that he really also
came from the Father. At that moment, the glory
of the Father fully breaks through upon him; then
he is complete revelation, revealing God as Father,
and by that same token, himself as Son, so that
who sees him sees the Father. This moment in which
the glory of the Father breaks through upon Jesus
is, for John, really the hour of his death, the hour
in which Jesus goes over from this world to the
Father. Elevation on the cross is elevation to glory.
This breakthrough of God's glory in Jesus' death is
eminently the revelation of his origin. Only then
does full light shine over his mission, origin and
nature. This does not alter the fact that his glory,
possessed from all eternity, occasionally breaks·
through, albeit in a veiled way, during his life —
diffused as the sun pressing its light through a bank
of mist. After the first Cana miracle, it is stated that
Jesus revealed his glory to his disciples who believed
(2:11). The raising of Lazarus, the last miracle, serves
also to show the glory of the Son of God (11:4). Within the framework of these two the meaning of the
other signs must also be judged. Here the difference
of accent between John's and the syoptic interpretation of miracles comes most sharply to light. In the
synoptics, they are, above all, signs of the coming
of the Kingdom insofar as this is not detached from
the person of Christ. For John, a miracle points

first to the person of Jesus himself, and hands on to
believers the key to the mystery of his being.

Miracles in John's gospel are called "signs" or
"works."[17] This does not mean that every sign or
work is a miracle, but only that miracles belong in
these categories. Although in the synoptics the
"sign" character belongs to miracles — because of
their reference to the presentation and status of the
Kingdom as well as to the power and authority of
Christ — they are seldom called signs, but rather
"powers" or "works of power." John's use of miracle
as "sign" is, on the other hand, noticeably frequent.
Sixteen times in the first twelve chapters (the public
life) the word "sign" is found. It begins with the
Cana miracle which brings the disciples to belief
(2:11); this is followed immediately by the Jewish
demands for a sign (2:18). From this moment on
the sign begins to effect a division of minds. It
evokes uneasiness, provokes disputes, generates
hatred, and leads finally, after the raising of Lazarus,
to the capture of Jesus and his condemnation.

In this use of the word John clearly distinguishes
himself from the synoptics. He is not especially
original, for the Old Testament also presents miracles
as signs of revelation and calls them so. Apart from
this, it is not only terminology which John has in
common with the Old Testament. The mention of
signs is itself a clear reference to the Old Testament
parade of miracle facts; the stereotyped Judaic-
rabbinic request for legitimation through signs also
is very old.

2. The "signs" of the Messiah

a. Miracles as legitimation

Jewish requests for signs as proof of authenticity developed into a sickly habit. Paul sees the Greeks as people who seek wisdom; he characterizes the Jews as a people demanding signs (1 Cor. 1:22). The synoptics (Mk. 8:12; Mt. 12:39; 16:4; Lk. 1:29) and John confirm Paul's observation. Christ scarcely appears, before the demand is made: "What sign have you to show us for doing this?" (2:18). When later he explicitly appeals to their consciences they ask: "Then what sign do you do that we may see, and believe you?" (6:30). Reproachfully, and with a touch of irony, Christ himself typified them: "Unless you see signs and wonders, you will not believe" (4:48).

This negative attitude of the Jews does not alter the fact that the sign is really a touchstone for authentic mission; along with this it is a guarantee of human faith in his mission. In fact, many believe in him to a certain extent by virtue of the signs (2:23). Nicodemus bears witness that Jesus, through his signs, is for him the teacher who comes from God (3:2). The miracle of the bread is guarantee for the multitude that he is the prophet who has come into the world (6:14). The abundance of his miracles becomes a sign of his Messianic mission: "When the Christ appears, will he do more signs than this man has done?" (7:31). Healing brings the man born blind to the conviction that Jesus cannot be a sinner, as the pharisees suggest, but that he is a holy and re-

ligious man who is heard because God is with him
(9:29-33). The raising of Lazarus too, includes this
import: "That they may believe that thou didst send
me" (11:42). Because he performed this sign, the
people went out to meet him, crying "Blessed is he
who comes in the name of the Lord, even the King
of Israel" (12:18).

b. Miracles as symbol of the Messianic richness of life

A sign serves as a credential which the divine
messenger gives to the people. It is more. At the
same time it reveals the nature of the mission with
which Jesus is charged. It refers to the supermun-
dane reality which Jesus reveals — the reality in
which he wants people to share. The changing of
water into wine, the miracle of the bread, the healings, and the raising of Lazarus are all facts with
a deeper, supernatural background. They allude to
the new beginning, the new salvific economy, superior to the old. They are the **actes de preésence** of
Messianic salvation, works of the Messiah. The manner in which the fourth evangelist effects this shows
how much his intention differs from that of the
synoptics. What for them is the ultimate object,
John takes as a first phase. For him the miracle
points through the Messianic function to the person
who performs it, and finds there the origin and
explantory ground for the entire salvific action of
God.[18] "But these signs are written that you may
believe that Jesus is the Christ, the Son of God, and
believing, you may have life in his name" (20:30-31).

"Son of God," in John's terminology, is not a synonym for "the Christ"; it indicates divine Sonship in the strict sense of the word. By placing both terms after one another John points out how miracles should be accepted: they lead man through a development of faith which brings him by way of belief in the mission and function of Christ to faith in what this person really is — the Son of God. Only then is this faith life-giving. The first dimension of the miracle is its Messianic character. John seeks, as do the others, legitimation in the fulfillment of Scripture; but, unlike Matthew, he does not accomplish this by formal quotation of prophetic texts. His argument is more subtle; he does not explicitly place text and fulfillment side by side, but he constantly uses the Old Testament as a point of reference, by pouring new situations and events into the mold of old facts, and by re-using certain literary characteristics, suggesting subtle likenesses, etc.

Such a procedure is not foreign to the Old Testament. The end time is a reproduction of the beginning which it restores. The situation which prevailed in paradise returns, in more ideal form, in the description of the final time. Messianic redemption too is prefigured by the deliverance from Egypt. It is therefore not surprising that John takes the theme of Exodus in the description of Jesus' Messianic appearance — the more so since he sees his whole person and mission under the sign of Exodus: his leaving the world and entrance into the glory of the Father. Are there any indications for this?

As mentioned earlier, the time of Exodus was rich
in signs. The word itself returns regularly in the
Books of Exodus, Numbers and Deouteronomy; only
John's gospel, as a "book of signs," can compare
to these. A number of like literary characteristics
are observable; linking of words with signs underlines the relationship between the Mosaic books and
the gospel of John. It would lead us too far afield
to treat these literary parallels here.[19] Of greater
importance are some of the associations which determine the trend of the narratives: God performed
miracle upon miracle before Pharaoh and also before
his chosen people. Yahweh calls the generation of
Exodus the generation which has seen his glory and
the signs he performed in Egypt and in the desert
(Num. 14:22). But Pharaoh was hard-hearted (Ex.
7:13) and the people of Israel refused to believe in
spite of the signs (Num. 14:11).

A similar situation becomes instantly clear in
John's gospel. In Cana, Jesus begins the series of
his signs and they reveal his glory (2:11). The signs
follow one another (11:42; 20:30), but he finds only
stubborn unbelief (12:37). To an indirect quotation
from Numbers 14:11, John adds two explicit ques-
tions from Isaiah: "Who has believed what we have
heard? And to whom has the arm of the Lord been
revealed?" (Is. 53:1). The strong arm of the Lord
is a term frequently used in Deuteronomy (cf. 4:34;
7:19; 11:2; 26:8) and means the performer of signs
and miracles. Another quotation (Is. 6:9) mentions
blindness of the eyes and hardening of the hearts

— a reproach also heard in Deuteronomy: "You have
seen all that the Lord did before your eyes in the
land of Egypt, to Pharaoh and to all his servants,
and to all his land, the great trials which your eyes
saw, the signs and those great wonders: but to this
day, the Lord has not given you a mind to understand, or eyes to see, or ears to hear" (Deut. 29:2-4).
And just as Deuteronomy closes with the words that
never again has there been a prophet in Israel like
Moses, who through Yahweh performed his signs
in the sight of Israel (Deut. 34:11-12), so the evangelist ends in the same vein, that Jesus did all these
signs in the sight of his disciples (20:30).

Does not this surprising similarity indicate in
broad outline that the signs from Exodus, deeply
written in the memory of Israel, not only happened
in days long ago but, as was hoped for in the future,
are actually taking place here and now? And that
they reveal, more perfectly than of old, the glory
of God, his remarkable demonstration of power for
the redemption of the world? An inventory of the
signs themselves will confirm this supposition and
its primeval indication!

A sign which fittingly recalls the wonderful past
is the miracle of the bread. The similarity and
radical affinity with the manna in the desert is very
clear. Although John has this miracle story in common with the synoptics, there are some differences.
The synoptics give as motive for the miracle the
fact that Jesus begins to instruct the people from
a feeling of compassion for their spiritual state, and

keeps them so long that the possibility of obtaining
food becomes difficult (Mk. 6:36). In the second
multiplication of the bread, the compassion is even
more closely coupled with the miracle. The instruction has taken so long that without precautionary
measures the physical condition of the people could
be in danger: "I have compassion on the crowd, because they have been with me now three days, and
have nothing to eat, and if I send them away hungry
to their homes, they will faint on the way" (Mk.
8:2-3).

John mentions that the multitude followed Jesus
because they had seen the miracles he had done for
the sick. There is no mention of instruction. There is
reason to perform a miracle because of the physically
dangerous situation which had occurred. Hence,
without introduction, Jesus begins: "How are we to
buy bread, so that these people may eat?" It seems
that there is no other reason than his will to provide
food. Naturally this is no whim or arbitrary decision.
But what then is the meaning? As will be shown
later, Christ through this sign wanted to focus attention of the Jews upon the nature of his mission and
his Person. He intended a correct orientation to
the fact that they followed him because of signs.
He did this through the miracle of the bread in
the desert shortly before the Paschal Feast. Naturally, mention of time requires first of all that the
exact moment in which this miracle happened be
fixed. This is done to preclude a purely symbolic
interpretation of the facts. But beside its chron-

ological interest, this moment of time also recalls the Exodus from Egypt and thus hints at a relationship. Precisely by way of this parallel the miracle can be understood as a sign of the Messiah. For it is common knowledge in Judaic tradition that the manna miracle will be repeated in Messianic times. In fact the "bread" miracle really arouses the conjecture that Jesus is the Messiah (6:14-15). The miracle serves less therefore to satisfy the hunger of the crowd as is the case in the synoptics, than indeed to reveal Jesus as the Messiah.

The multiplication of the bread is coupled with a second miracle that surpasses the rain of manna. During the passage through the desert, the Jews were allowed to gather manna sufficient for the needs of one day; more than this decayed. Therefore, the Israelites were forbidden to lay up a store (Ex. 16:16-20). Here, however, Jesus commanded them to gather up what was left. Properly speaking, one cannot say left, or leavings, or remainder: the amount of unconsumed bread greatly surpasses the sparse quantity available in the beginning. This superfluity is accentuated to direct the expectation of the people to the person of the Messiah. This is the fulfillment of the abundance which would become Israel's share after taking possession of the Promised Land. Full of meaning also is the fact that the superfluous bread is gathered so that it might not be lost. This bread serves not only the five thousand, but also all who shall come after them. This bread which does not perish and is there in

abundance for every one in need of it points to the
food and life of the end time, and therefore to the
Eucharistic Bread. The result of this miracle is dis-
appointing to Jesus. The people are certainly wild
and enthusiastic but their enthusiasm is a reaction
only to their own profit. Though they interpret the
miracle as the Messiah's, this nevertheless is not
from appreciation for the Messiah but for the bread:
"I say to you, you seek me, not because you saw
signs, but because you ate your fill of the loaves"
(6:26).

The "Wine Miracle" in Cana shows many aspects
of similarity with the multiplication of the bread in
the desert. But while Jesus himself explained the
sign value of the miracle of the bread with a subsequent discourse, the evangelists here mentions only
in a general way that the miracle serves as revelation
of his glory. This however is not typical only of
the wine miracle; it fixes the direction of all other
miracle signs mentioned. The specific sign-value
remains unmentioned. It is necessary therefore, in
trying to determine this, not to proceed too hastily.[20]

Of what does the wine remind us? The theme of
wine occurs frequently in the Old Testament. Except
for sporadic exceptions, its meaning is positive and
optimistic. Wine is part of a triad — corn, wine, oil
— the three necessities of man's life, and benevolent
gifts of God: "That he may bring forth food from
the earth, and wine to gladden the heart of man,
oil to make his face shine, and bread to strengthen
man's heart" (Ps. 104:14-15). Abundance of corn,

wine and oil is a sign of welfare and is seen as a
result of fidelity to God's covenant (Deut. 7:12-13).
Israel's infidelity makes them realize that God shall
not leave them grain, wine or oil (Deut. 28:51;
Hosea 2:11). The close connection between wine,
promised land and covenant, is also the theme of
the prophets, who throw light upon the Messianic
reparation and the contingent fidelity of the people
to the covenant. Jeremias sings of Israel's future
happiness with the words: "They shall come and
sing aloud on the height of Sion and they shall be
radiant over the goodness of the Lord, over the
grain, the wine and the oil . . ." (Jer. 31:12; cf. Is.
62:8). And Amos: "Behold the days are coming, says
the Lord, when the ploughman shall overtake the
reaper, and the treader of grapes him who sows
the seeds; the mountains shall drip sweet wine, and
all the hills shall flow with it" (Amos 9:13).

This theme is seriously overworked in the apocry-
phal literature; abundance of grain and wine takes
on unheard of proportions. Further, two texts are
especially important, because of their direct or indirect Messianic tenor. Isaac give Jacob the blessing which makes him lord over the peoples and
enriches him with plenty of grain and wine (Gen.
27:28-37). Isaac's blessing of Jacob passes on from
him to the seed of Judah: "Binding his foal to the
vine, and his ass's colt to the choice vine, he washes
his garments in wine and his vesture in the blood
of grapes; his eyes shall be red with wine and his
teeth shall be white with milk" (Gen. 49:10-12).

A second aspect associated with this theme of wine is gladness. Psalm 104 and the Book of Judges 9:13 briefly indicate this. The Book of Sirach elaborates this opinion: Wine is for man the water of life, if he drinks moderately. What is life without wine? It was created in the beginning for happiness! If drunk with moderation wine is joy for the heart, happiness and pleasure (Sirach 31:27-28).

One can say this about wine: it is the result as well as the sign of God's blessing. Mention of it therefore can be turned into the framework of future reparation. Its abundance is a sign of God's boundless grace and people's endless joy in the messianic era.

New Testament symbolism of wine was adaptable to the figure of banquet or wedding feast; only in Cana does it play a central part. It is not very difficult to determine the sign value of this miracle. As was the case in the miracle of the bread, the evangelist here draws attention to abundance. He estimates that the capacity of the water pots is about ten to fifteen gallons. Why this abundance if not to indicate that wine would be plentiful at this wedding feast, and that others could also enjoy it? The wine in Cana, abundant in quantity and of eminently excellent quality is an indication of the superabundant luxury of the time of salvation, which dawns with Christ's death. As such, this wonder at the same time throws light on his Messianic dignity.

Are we allowed to see in the Cana wine an indication of the Eucharistic wine, as the bread miracle is the prefiguration of the Eucharistic bread? The latter is confirmed in Scripture itself, the first is not; this does not mean that we must deny it outright.

Could not the change of water into wine in the stone pots used for cleansing, be a symbol of the redemption of the old economy by the new one which surpasses it in grace? This too is more than can be proved! Let us rather stay with the common opinion. Like the multiplication of the bread, the wine miracle points to the person of the Messiah and the abundance and inexhaustibility of the Messianic era. It is possible that the wine miracle, just like the Old Testament water miracle, alludes to the miraculous abundance which quenched Israel's thirst in the desert. Not only Exodus but the entire prophetic prognosis present miracles as Messianic signs.

There are still "other miracles" in John's gospel which are related to one another. They are the healing of the son of the centurion, the healing of the lame man, and the raising of Lazarus. These demonstrate Jesus' power over life and death.

As with the synoptics, one can here see once more that deliverance from illness and death is an indication of eschatological salvation and of recognition of the Messiah as the one who has dominion over death. This is Messianic work with a specific sign value.

In all three passages John underlines the might

of Jesus' life-bringing word. The son of the courtier is dying. When Jesus begins to reproach the crowd meeting him, the father can no longer restrain his impatience and insists: "Sir, come down before my son dies!" (4:49). Jesus heals the boy from a distance by his word: "Go, your son will live" (4:50). The healing of the lame man is a parallel case. For thirty-eight years his existence was more like death than life, without hope of a cure. Here too, one single word: "Rise, take up your pallet and walk" (5:8), and immediate effect follows. In the raising of Lazarus the power of Jesus' word reveals itself in full splendor. A dead person, three days in the grave, is raised by the loud cry: "Lazarus, come out" (11:43).

We see three hopeless cases: a dying child, a paralytic for thirty-eight years, a corpse of three days; one single word, and an immediate effect. This is not mere happenstance; there is also an interior connection. The raising of Lazarus is the full unfolding of what is demonstrated in the two healings: Jesus' victory over death. The child, for all practical purposes, is called back from death; the restoration of the partially extinguished life of the paralytic is a promise and proof of the definitive resurrection which the same Christ in his full Messianic function shall bring about by a single word (5:28-29). Thus these miracles underline the soteriological meaning of Jesus' mission. As restoration of physical life they are already an anticipatory fulfillment of Jesus' own testimony: "I am the resurrection and the life" (11:25). But the fringe value of the miracle allows for yet further advance. This same tendency is present in the healing of the man born blind. John follows the established process: human need, direct healing, verification by the outer world. This is to indicate that the healing is a real miracle. But the specific sign value does not go unrecorded. The key expression is: "I am the light of the world."

9:5 reads: "As long as I am in the world, I am the light of the world." In 8:12, "I am the light of the world. He who follows me, will not walk in darkness but will have the light of life."

The healing of the blind man, as mentioned in the synoptics, belongs to the Messianic time. It is simultaneously a symbol for a spiritual turning to, and opening up to, God. John suggests even more. Walking in the light recalls the desert event when Israel marched behind the fire column and was protected and saved by it (Ex. 13; Ps. 78:14; 105:39). This phenomenon recurs in the Messianic time when God once more takes into his hands the restoration of Israel and gives a new demonstration of his power. This light is the salvation and life of the people whom God calls in the end time. Even the gentiles take part in it (Is. 8:23-29; 40:3-11; 60). As life triumphs over death, so light edges out darkness. The cited healing of the blind man is a sign of this triumph of the light. As one who comes to the light he is also a prototype of the new people of God who believes in Jesus as the light of divine revelation and salvation. From belief in him, the blind man came to see in a new way; others who were under the illusion of seeing became blind. Jesus himself explicitly unveils this symbol value of the miracle (9:39).

Conclusion: Exegetes correctly call the first part of John's gospel "the book of signs" because in many ways it pre-eminently recalls the time of signs in the Old Testament. It is however not clear whether the separate miracles, one by one, reflect the signs of Exodus. This shows up most strikingly in regard to the miracle of the bread. The healing of the man born blind can, because of Christ's affirmation, be connected with the light miracle of the desert. The wine miracle is a neat parallel with the wondrous abundance of water which Moses brought from the rock, even though a wider context is productive of a more satisfactory result. In the desert a healing takes place for Israel too, through looking up to the sign of the brass serpent. At the same time death, which God sends Israel as a punishment, is averted through the intervention of Aaron and Moses. But that these latter events play any part in John's typology is doubtful; they certainly are not convincingly proved.[21] Memories of Exodus need not be recalled as much through a precise similarity of signs as through their abundance and grandeur.

3. The "works" of the Son of Man

a. Son of Man and Son of God

Jesus' miracles are the signs of the Messianic time and therefore bear salvific characteristics. Simultaneously, they possess a dimension of the end time.

Because Old Testament expectations are still valid
for the gospels, inception of the Messianic time
would also include the final time. The miracles of
Jesus therefore carry this implication. John emphat-
ically touches on this in separate instances. The
wine miracle and the multiplication of the bread
point to eschatological abundance which, when the
time is ripe, will become reality. Just as the wine
does not run out and the bread does not perish, so
the light acquired by the blind is eternal, and the
healings, seen in perspective of the raising of Lazarus,
are a guarantee of the life that remains forever. Thus
miracles point to that phase of salvation of which
it is written: "They shall hunger no more, neither
thirst no more" (Rev. 7:16). "He will wipe away
every tear from their eyes, and death shall be no
more: neither shall there be mourning nor crying
nor pain" (id. 21:4); "And night shall be no more;
they need no light of lamp or sun, for the Lord God
will be their light and they shall reign for ever and
ever" (id. 22:5).

The signs which directly reveal the Messiah are,
because of their eschatological quality, at the same
time the proclamation of the definitive salvific situation which will begin with the end of this world.
This is an act of God's power which encompasses
the raising of the dead and judgment. Both are
closely related, because the manner in which the
life-giving power of God's word touches man is
clearly the effect of an efficacious judgment. Through
this act of power God's work is accomplished for

the salvation of the world. Jesus does not consider himself solely as an arbitrary messenger from God, but as the one who, vested with judicial power, has come to accomplish the will of the Father concerning the end time. Hence he calls himself the Son of Man — he who is considered by Judaic tradition as the judge who shall carry out the final judgment in the name of Yahweh.

John does not stop here. Without prior notice, the title "Son of Man" transmutes into "Son of God." This means that he who calls himself "Son of Man" is not restricted by man but is also the Son of God. This sonship is of such a nature that he who calls God his Father manifests this intimacy of life-unity in word and being (Jn. 5:16-18; 10:38).

The final judgment and the resurrection, the destruction of satan, death and sin, are the great works which the Father performs through the Son. But other performances during Jesus' life can also be called "works" because they propel, as it were, to the final operations of the Son of Man at the end time. Mriacles too must be seen on this plane. They serve as testimony for the Messiah, but they also have for their object inducement to faith in the Son of God (Jn. 20:31). This is the new and proper dimension which the miracle holds for John: not to be understood as solely a Messianic work, but as the working of the Father through his Son in the truest sense of the word. The miracle as "work" indicates an eschatological dimension which is not noticed by the Jews. For although the eschatological stamp is visible in the Messianic sign, it does not include **ipso facto** that Jesus has a function of the final end itself. And it is precisely to this that his miracle as "work" means to point. Whoever refuses to accept this cannot come to the faith intended by the miracle. For that reason, miracles as a grace of God simultaneously include judgment. Let us trace this developed perspective in separate miracles.

b. Separate miracles and their revelation of the Son of God

After the wine miracle, the evangelist writes: "This was the first of his signs, Jesus did at Cana in Galilee, and manifested his glory; and his disciples believed in him" (Jn. 2:11). What does John mean by "his glory?" The origin of this word leads us back to the Old Testament. The glory is God's essence, God's being insofar as it manifests and shows itself to man. It is an anticipation of the divine. This manifestation shall fall to man's lot in full only after this life, when he stands face to face with God. It is therefore a salvific reality essentially eschatological. John brings this glory into his gospel as an expression of the divine and relates it to the person of Christ (Jn. 12:40). Christ prays explicitly that the Father may give him the glory which he possessed from the beginning. This becomes his in the hour of his Passion, in his passage from the world to his Father. This means that it is now veiled, accessible only to those who see in a divine way — through supernatural faith. Only thus does the hidden Son of Man become Son "in glory."

John explicitly mentions that the disciples belong to those who saw his glory — that this miracle led them to Jesus as the Son of God.

The evangelist depended on help from the Old Testament to represent the mysterious unity between Father and Son which is revealed in the miracles. This he did by means of the notion "glory." Miracles of the gospel manifest the glory of Jesus in the same way as those of the Old Testament revealed the glory of Yahweh. This means that the glory of Yahweh is with us in Jesus Christ. This is why the eschatology of miracles cannot be understood except through faith in the Incarnation. The signs are, for John, the works of the Word made Flesh among us. They are the signs of the Son of God, who as Son of Man is involved in the work of God at the end time — giving eternal life to the world.

The healing of the lame man is especially relevant to the works of the Son of Man at the end time. This healing, which occurs on the Sabbath, thereby includes an incident with the scribes. Jesus justifies himself: "My Father is working still and I am working" (Jn. 5:17). Although God rested from his creative activity on the seventh day (according to Judaic theology) he continues to exercise his dominion over life and death. The healing of the lame man belongs to the judicial activity of Yahweh. Jesus' reference to the power over life and forgiveness of sins which the Father has allotted to him (Jn. 5:13), indeed brings the Jews to the right conclusion: "He makes himself equal to God" (5:18). In order that no one will doubt the correctness of this conclusion, he adds to it by making the true eschatological judicial function of Yahweh — judgment and control over resurrection from the dead — his own: "For as the Father raises the dead and gives them life, so also the Son gives life to whom he will" (5:21). And "He has given him authority to execute judgment, because he is the Son of Man" (5:27). This healing of the lame man is only the beginning of his great work. While the courtier believes in the life-giving power of Jesus' word, which as Yahweh's word never fails in effect, the authorities of Jerusalem close their eyes to the light which is to reveal him.

That miracles foster faith in the Son of Man and the Son of God is even more accentuated in the following signs. Because of the multiplication of the bread, Christ calls himself The Bread of Life (6:35). Precisely because he is the Light (8:12; 9:5), he heals the man born blind; and before he raises Lazarus, he professes that he is the resurrection and the life (11:25). Revelation of the eschatological Son of Man and the incarnate Son of God is here made in one affirmation. He not only gives bread, light and life, but he **is** these. Miracles manifest not only his salvation function, but himself as salvific gift. And he can be this only because he possesses the same divine life as the Father himself, and can therefore impart it to others. References which follow from the miracles — the wine which does not run out, the bread which does not perish, the light which is eternal, the life which is immortal — are in

the deepest sense references made to himself. He
says: "I am the bread, the light and the life." He
insists that he is for Israel and the world what
Yahweh was for Israel. As Messiah, he is therefore
not merely a new Moses who through God's power
performs the miracles of the Exodus and even
greater ones. He is identical with the God of the
Exodus. The bearer of the Messianic function is the
Son of God himself. Consequently, who believes in
him has life.

4. Unbelief

"These miracles are written that you may believe."
This contrasts paradoxically with the fact that the
"Book of Signs" closes with the perplexing words:
"Though he had done so many signs before them
(the Jews), yet they did not believe him" (Jn. 12:37).
Real faith is displayed only by the disciples (2:11),
the courtier who believed along with his whole
family (4:54), the man born blind who resolutely
defended him against his aggressors, and the sisters
of Lazarus. In the other cases, John first mentions
that miracles bring about certain effects. But Christ
sees in this only an unreliable enthusiasm, directed
too much to earthly realities and not to his own
person. Thus the initial optimism is cruelly disrupted:
the signs in the end become a rebuff. We know the
cause. If the person of Christ is revealed only to him
who believes, then there is a seeing of signs that is
not true faith. This can lead to obduration of mind
and blindness of heart. John quotes the prophetic
words from the Book of Isaiah: "He has blinded

their eyes and hardened their hearts, lest they should see with their eyes and perceive with their hearts and turn for me to heal them" (Jn. 12:40).

The crowd saw the signs, but usually in the light of their own material concerns and political dreams. Others saw signs but were afraid to confess their faith for fear of the Pharisees (Jn. 12:42). Nicodemus is too rationalistic and cannot risk the leap from his insights into the obscurity of belief (3:2-12). The Samaritan woman vacillates (Jn. 4:29). The pharisees on the other hand are blinded through hatred. Their seeing of the signs ends in a complete revolt against God himself. The rebuff of the sign lies in this: it has not led the Jews to the "works." He who would see the miracle as "work" would believe in the Son of God.

5. Life in his Name

It is understandable that, after the glorification of Christ, the interest of the evangelist should turn more and more to possession of him. The message concerning the coming of the Kingdom gives way to a consciousness of newly acquired life; this life by its very nature is directed toward its completion at the end time. That which is indicated by miracles as eschatological grace is already present in Christ: "I am the bread of life, the eternal light, the resurrection." In this way the evangelist ties together Jesus' miracles and their meaning for all men. In comparison with the first disciples, every generation which has not known the historical Jesus is impoverished. Faith is essential if there is to be communion in eternal life.

Precisely because of the strong symbolism attached to the miracles of Jesus, a question is posed: If miracles are not what sacraments are for us, what was their function in Jesus' days? Therefore, in conclusion, we consider the sacrament in its relation to the miracle.

a. Sacrament

"He shall come back as he is risen." These words from the Acts also form the theme of John wherever he speaks of the Son of Man. Between ascension and parousia the Church lives as a community of the faithful drawing strength from Christ's past earthly life and hopefully looking forward to his inseparable presence in their lives after the parousia. Christian life is however more than just living from a memory toward an expectation. Christ, by his resurrection from the dead, is a presence through his Spirit in the Church. This presence is a real existence, communicated by the signs he himself has given — the sacraments. The Twelve, through direct contact with him received that which the faithful after them obtain through baptism: forgiveness of sins and eternal life. In other words, during his earthly life, Jesus led his disciples directly into the salvific economy. After his ascent to the Father, every one — because the Incarnation is not a recurring event — is led into the same salvation through baptism in his name. So the faithful come to a personal fellowship with Christ, become "One Body" with him.

This is also true of the Eucharist. As long as Jesus himself was present with his diciples, the Eucharistic celebration has no meaning. This is why this sign was instituted only at the end of his life. Nor will the Eucharist any longer be necessary in the coming Kingdom; a new spiritual banquet will then unite the Lord with his people. Through the Eucharist there is a fellowship between Christ and his faithful as strong as that which obtained between him and his disciples. This parallel is strongly emphasized by John. The Word is made Flesh and has presented life to the world. After this the Son is again taken up into the glory of the Father. But what he gave his disciples in the time of the Incarnation, this he gives to the faithful of all generations through the Eucharist which is his Flesh and Blood. This sacramental fellowship is as real and active as is the fellowship between Jesus and his disciples.

b. Miracle-sacrament relationship

Miracles are precursors of the Kingdom. They announce a redemption which in its integral fulfillment is eschatological in nature. They therefore occurred all through the history of salvation. The wonders which accompanied Israel's deliverance from Egypt were signs of coming salvation. In the New Testament, Jesus' resurrection is the greatest miracle, the sign **par excellence** of the nearness and in a certain sense the already-presence of the Kingdom. Through the Holy Spirit the salvific reality of the Incarnation

remains present in history; through him the powers
of the coming age are already active in it. But,
though strengthened by the Spirit, the Church is
not yet in possession of the **dynamis,** the irresistible
divine force which pertains only to the Kingdom of
God. The Church is still assailed by the powers of
the enemy, and her members are still subject to
the blows of the last and worst enemy — death.
Death can be destroyed only at the end of time.
The Church is not yet the Kingdom. Miracles point
to this; they will take place as long as the Kingdom
is still coming.

Seen historically, with salvation as the point of
reference, miracles are less needed now than before
Pentecost because the Church itself has become
the sign of the Kingdom. But they do take place
nevertheless, to show that salvific history, although
it has entered upon its last phase, has not yet come
to completion. As long as the end has not become
a total reality for all, miracles, pointing to this end
time and announcing its power, will occur.

The sacraments also are signs that the Lord is
really present in his Church. Whereas miracles
belong to all periods of salvation history, this is not
true of the sacraments. These belong to the last
period of salvific history. In the Old Testament we
cannot speak of sacraments in the strict and proper
sense. They are signs of Christ's presence while he
is bodily absent. They can therefore exist only
within the space of time bordered by his resurrection

(ascension) and the parousia. Through them Christ is present under a form made uniquely possible between ascension and parousia, but no less real than during his earthly life. Sacraments are the contact reality within which Christ imparts his life to the Church and thus to the world.

During his lifetime, Jesus performed miracles. They functioned as portents of the beginning of the Christological Kingdom; they accompanied the earthly presence and action of the Messiah. The same situation remains also for the Church. Sacrament does not abrogate miracle. Their lasting parallelism in the Church supports the Christian viewpoint that salvation is historical as well as eschatological. Sacraments re-present the historical act of Christ's death for forgiveness of sins and eternal life for mankind. They testify that the faithful, because of their existential reality, possess forgiveness of sins and life in Christ. They confirm that the Lord has already come and that he remains with his people to make them share his life in the Church.

Miracles, on the other hand, announce eschatological fulfillment, redemption of the body, resurrection on the last day. They announce the still expected Kingdom in power and glory. Certainly, miracle and sacrament depend on the same salvation event; the evangelists rightly identifies the feeding of the five thousand as a sign of the Eucharistic sacrament. But miracle and sacrament allow for no more distinction than do Church and Kingdom. Just as the existence of the Church does not abolish hope in what is to come, so the sacrament does not replace the miracle. Sacrament and miracle stand in the same relationship as Church and Kingdom.

BIBLIOGRAPHY

1. R. Guardini: *Wonder en teken* (hilversum 1959); P. Schoonenberg: *Het geloof van ons doopsel*, II (s' Hertogenbosch) p. 149; B. v. Leuven: "Wonder en natuurorde," in *Werkgenootschap Kath. Theol.* (1953) pp. 5-13.

2. W. Eichrodt; *Theologie des Alten Testamentes*, II (Berlin 1950) pp. 77-87.

3. Th. C. Vriezen; *Hoofdlijnen der theolgie van het Oude Testament.* (Wageningen 1954) p. 146.

4. Vriezen: op. cit. p. 147.

5. Guardini, op cit. p. 34.

6. G. Von Rad; *Theologie des Alten Testaments* 1 (Munich 1957) pp. 177-181.

7. Von Rad: op. cit. pp. 279-284.

8. Guardini: op. cit. pp. 36-45.

9. R. Schnackenburg: *Gottes Herrschaft und Reich* (Freiburg 1959) pp. 1-48.

10. For the entire chapter: A. Richardson: *The Miracle Stories of the Gospels.* (London 1956).
L. Monden: *Het wonder* (Utrecht-Antwerp 1958) pp. 7-119.

11. Schnackenburg: op. cit. pp. 79-110.

12. Schoonenberg: op. cit. pp. 137-148; E. Walter: *Geloof, hoop en liefde in het Nieuwe Testament* (Bussum 1953) pp. 5-34.

13. G. Bouwman: "Kerygma en Didache" in: *Ned. Kath. Stemmen* (1957) pp. 177-184.

14. H. J. Held: "Matthaus als Interpret der Wundergeschichten," in: G. Bornkamn: *Ueberlieferungen und*

Auslegung im Matthausevangelium (Neukirchen 1960) pp. 155-289.

15. Since Jn. 21 goes beyond the structure of the Gospel and mentions events which took place after the Resurrection, we do not include the miraculous catch of fish (Jn. 21:1-4) in our account.

16. For this entire chapter: H. van den Bussche: *Het vierde evangelie* (Tielt 1959-1960).

17. Van den Bussche gives chapters 1-4 the title of the "Book of Signs" and 5-12 the "Book of Works."

18. L. Cerfaux: "Les miracles, signes messianiques de Jésus et eouvres de Dieu selon l'évangile de S. Jean" in: *L'Attente du Messie* (Brugge 1954) pp. 131-138; J. P. Charlier: "La notion de signe (semeion)) dans IV évangile" in: *Revue des Sciences Phil. et Théol.* (1959) pp. 434-448; C. H. Dodd: *The Interpretation of the Fourth Gospel* (Cambridge 1954).

19. Cf. D. Mallat: "Le semeion johanique" in: *Sacra Pagina* II (Paris-Gembloux 1959) pp. 209-218.

20. Cf. M. E. Boismard: *Du baptême à Cana* (Lectio Divina 18) pp. 133-165; A. Feuillet: "L'heure de Jésus at le signe de Cana," in: *Ephem. Theol. Lov.* 36 (1960) pp. 5-23.

21. G. Ziener: "Weisheitsbuch und Johannesevangelium," in: *Biblica* 38 (1957) pp. 396-418, makes connection between the exodus and the miracle narratives in the fourth gospel via the Book of Wisdom. Chapters 11, 16, 18.

22. W. Grossouw: *Bijbelse vroomheid* (Utrecht 1955) pp. 211-220: Sacramental signs; Ph. H. Menoud, "Miracle et Sacrament dans le N.T." in: *Verbum Caro* (1952) pp. 139-154.